CW01651547

KEY STAGE 2

Keeping healthy

Jacqueline Dineen

CAMBRIDGE
UNIVERSITY PRESS

Published by the Press Syndicate of the
University of Cambridge
The Pitt Building, Trumpington Street,
Cambridge CB2 1RP
40 West 20th Street, New York,
NY 10011-4211, USA
10 Stamford Road, Oakleigh,
Melbourne 3166, Australia

First published 1994

Designed by Guy Hooper and Pardoe Blacker Publishing Ltd, Shawlands Court, Newchapel Road, Lingfield, Surrey RH7 6BL
Illustrated by Annabelle Brend, Dawn Brend, Harry Clow, Charlotte Cruise, Chris Forsey, Nicholas Hall, Jenny Mumford, Viv Quillin and Gareth Wild

Printed in Great Britain at the University Press, Cambridge

A catalogue record for this book is available from the British Library

ISBN 0 521 39758 8

Acknowledgements

The author and publishers would like to thank Tony Cowie B Sc, BVSC, MRCVS for his help in the preparation of this book.

Publisher's note

The International League for the Protection of Horses (ILPH) are willing to supply a video and information pack, free of charge, to any school. Applications should be sent to the following address: HQ ILPH, Anne Colvin House, Snetterton, Norfolk NR16 2LR.

Photographic credits

t=top b=bottom c=centre l=left r=right
Cover: Science Photo Library

4 Bruce Coleman; 5 Solitaire Photographic; 6*t* Hilly Hoar ARPS, West Sussex College of Agriculture/ Brinsbury College; 6*b* NHPA; 8 Solitaire Photographic; 11 Trevor Hill; 13*t* Bruce Coleman; 13*b* Animal Photography; 16 Hilly Hoar ARPS, West Sussex College of Agriculture/Brinsbury College; 17*t* Chris Fairclough; 17*b* Bob Langrish; 18*t* ILPH; 19*t* RSPCA; 19*b* Bruce Coleman; 23*t* Bruce Coleman; 23*b* Chris Fairclough; 24 Science Photo Library; 27*t*, *b* Science Photo Library; 31 Chris Fairclough; 33*l* Science Photo Library; 33*t* Trevor Hill; 33*b* Science Photo Library; 35*t* NHPA; 35*bl* Science Photo Library; 35 Trevor Hill; 36 Science Photo Library; 37 Trevor Hill; 38 Science Photo Library; 39 Trevor Hill; 44*t* Trevor Hill; 44*b* Chris Fairclough; 46 Science Photo Library; 47 Chris Fairclough; 48*l* Chris Fairclough; 48*r* Science Photo Library; 49*tl* Science Photo Library; 49*bl* Chris Fairclough; 49*tr* Science Photo Library; 49*br* Mary Evans Picture Library; 53 ZEFA; 54*t* ZEFA; 54*b* Trevor Hill; 55 Trevor Hill; 57*l* Science Photo Library; 57*r* Science Photo Library; 58 Science Photo Library

Contents

Introduction	4
The vet	6
Preventing illness	8
Curing illness	10
Continuing the line	12
A day in the life of a vet	14
Into hospital	16
At an animal centre	18
At the zoo	20
Going to the doctor	24
Genetic illness	26
Other illnesses	28
Diagnosing an illness	32
Food poisoning	34
Treating illness	36
Drug abuse	38
A day in the life of a GP	40
Going to hospital	44
Seeing a specialist	46
The surgeon	48
Major surgery	50
What causes heart conditions?	52
After an operation	54
Transplant surgery	56
Blood groups	58
Getting better	60
Key words	62
Index	64

Introduction

What does 'keeping healthy' mean? Some people think that they are healthy if they are not ill. In fact, there is a big difference between not feeling ill and being really fit and well.

Find out more about the things you need to stay healthy in the *New Horizons* book, *Look you! Look me!*

Micro-organisms are very tiny living things, which can invade the body. **Bacteria**, **viruses** and **fungi** are micro-organisms.

All animals (and that includes you!) need certain things to stay healthy. They need a good **diet** which means eating the right mixture of foods. They also need water, sleep, relaxation and exercise.

A healthy body fights off illness more effectively than an unhealthy one. If you eat 'junk' food and never take any exercise, your body weakens. It cannot easily attack the **micro-organisms** that cause illness.

Vets and doctors

Healthy animals may become ill sometimes. Then they may need medical help. Veterinary surgeons help sick animals and doctors help sick people. Vets and doctors need similar skills to **diagnose** illnesses and cure them. They have to understand how the body works and what can go wrong with it. Once they have found out what is wrong, they have to try to put it right. They need to know all about medicines and what they do. They also try to prevent illness.

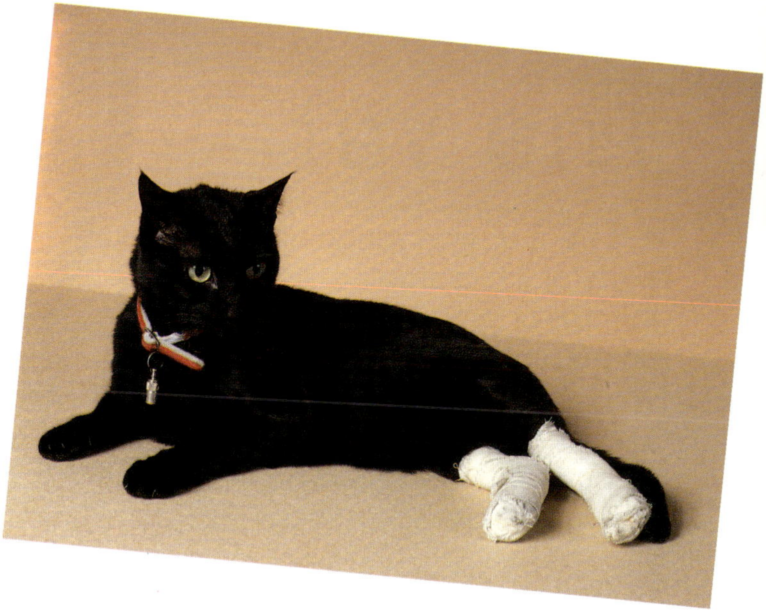

Animals may be wounded in accidents. Bones may be broken. Vets and doctors have to know how to treat wounds so that they heal. Broken bones have to be set so that they knit together properly.

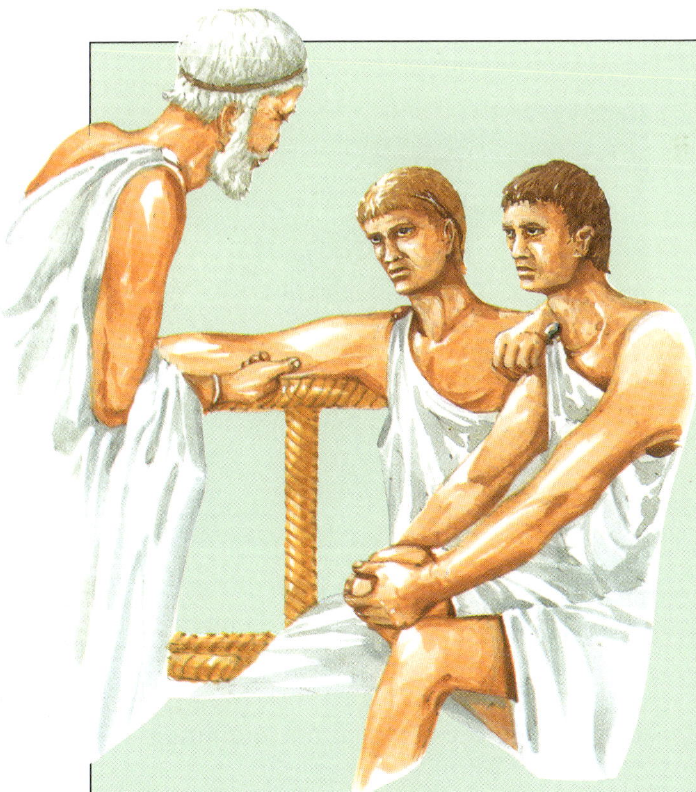

Hippocrates

Early people believed that illness was caused by the gods or by evil spirits. They thought they had to please the gods or spirits before an illness could be cured. In about 450 BC, a Greek man called Hippocrates suggested that illnesses could be diagnosed and treated by people. He set up a school of medicine on the Greek island of Kos. Doctors had to take the Hippocratic Oath. For this they promised to carry out their duties and treat the sick by the methods they had been taught. Doctors still have to take this oath before they can practise medicine.

More about: bones pp7 diet pp29, 54-55 micro-organisms pp10, 25, 35

The vet

Vets treat a wide range of animals. Many of the animals are farm animals or pets. Some vets treat zoo animals, or wild animals which have been injured. Different types of animals get different illnesses and the vet has to be able to diagnose and treat them all.

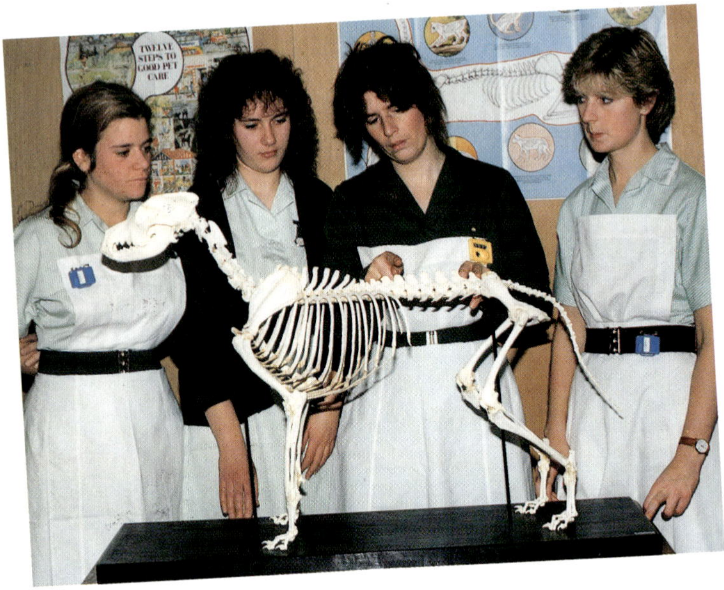

Vets have to know all about animals' bodies and what can go wrong with them. People who want to become vets have to train for at least five years.

Mammals' bodies

Many of the animals the vet sees are **mammals**. All mammals have the same organs. They have eyes to see and ears to hear and they have a heart, lungs, a liver and kidneys.

Find out more about mammals in the *New Horizons* book, *Life around us.*

Sometimes vets have to treat other types of animals such as birds. Birds have organs, blood and muscles. Their bones and feathers are light so that they can fly. What is the same about mammals and birds? What is different?

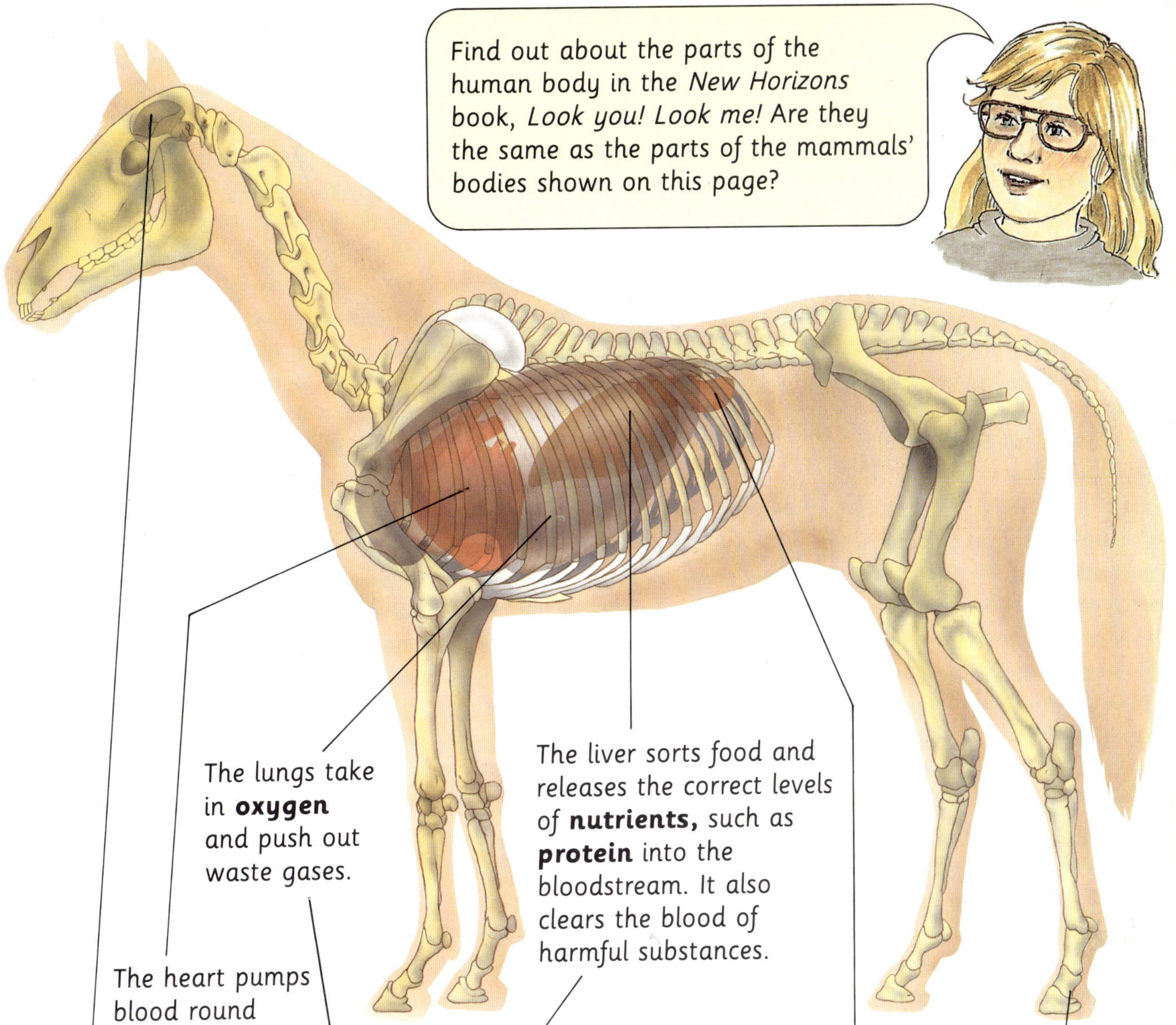

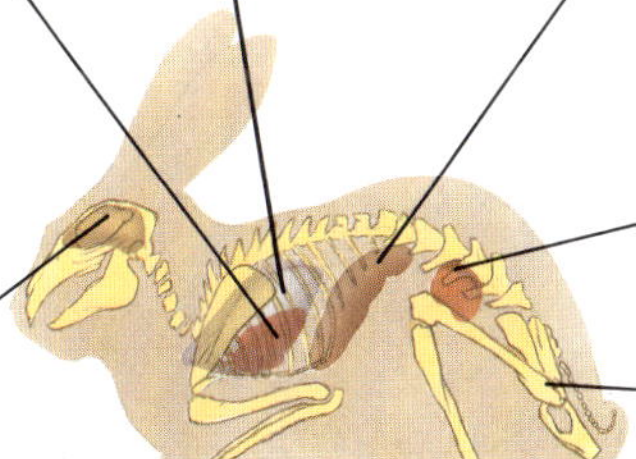

More about: birds pp19 kidneys pp50, 57 zoos pp20-23

Preventing illness

If animals are well looked after by their owners, many illnesses can be prevented. A healthy mammal has a glossy coat and bright eyes. It is neither too thin nor too fat.

Owners can keep their animals in good condition by making sure they have good food and plenty of exercise. They can also help to prevent their animals becoming ill.

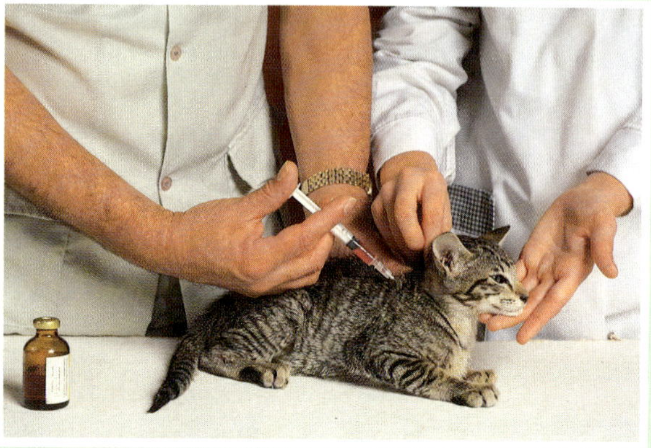

Feline infectious enteritis is a fatal illness for cats. A kitten should be vaccinated against it before it is three months old and kept away from other cats until then.

Vaccinations

Animals can pick up **infectious** diseases from other animals. Some of these diseases are **fatal**, but the vet can **vaccinate** animals against them. A vaccination is an injection which makes the body resistant to the disease.

Distemper is a disease which can affect dogs, foxes and some other animals. Puppies can be vaccinated against distemper at about 11 weeks old.

A new pet

A new pet should be examined by a vet to make sure that it is healthy.

Cats have delicate ears which easily become infected. The vet checks the kitten's ears carefully.

He looks at the eyes to make sure they are not dirty or runny. This can be a sign of infection.

Coping with parasites

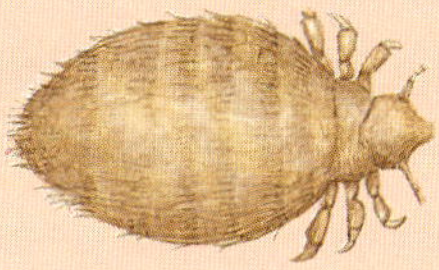
louse

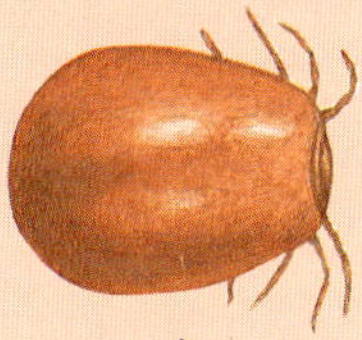
tick

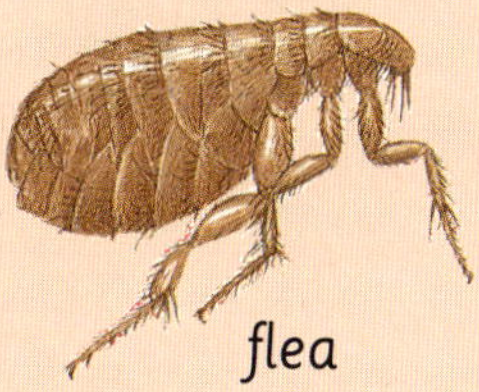
flea

Animals pick up **parasites** such as fleas, lice, ticks and worms. If the parasites are not dealt with quickly, the animal becomes **infested**. The vet treats the parasites with a powder or tablets. Fleas live on the animal's skin and make it itch, so the animal scratches itself a lot. If an animal has fleas, you will see black specks in its fur. You should treat the animal's coat with flea powder and comb it thoroughly. Lice are tiny. They lay their eggs in the animal's fur. Ticks are blood-suckers. Animals which live in the country are more likely to pick up ticks than town animals.

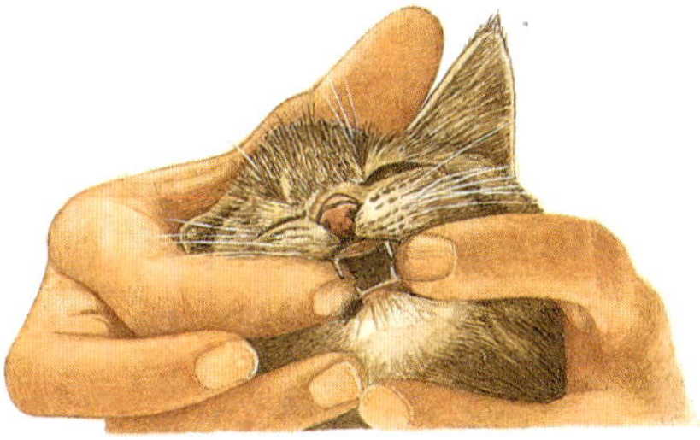

The kitten should have a full set of healthy milk teeth. These are small teeth which appear soon after the kitten is born. They drop out and are replaced by larger permanent teeth when the kitten is five or six months old.

The vet checks the kitten's coat for fleas and gives it a worming tablet to get rid of any worms.

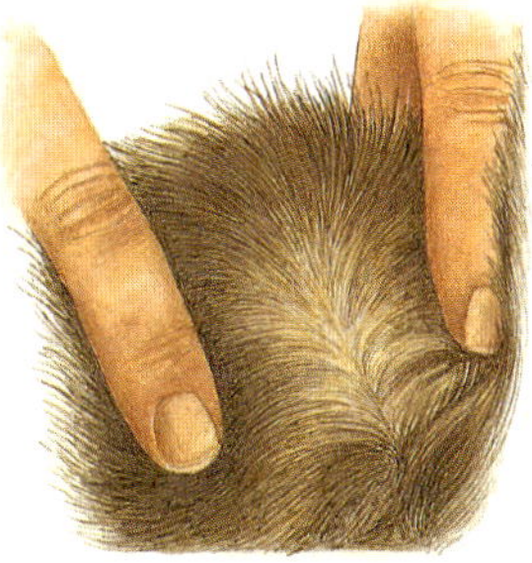

Sometimes, the vet trims claws that are too long and sharp. A cat normally keeps its own claws short by scratching a tree-trunk or a special scratching post bought from a pet shop.

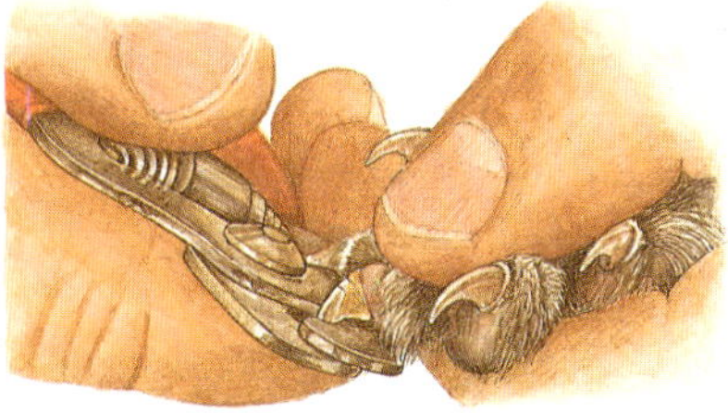

Did you know...?

Fleas spread by jumping from one animal to another. The common flea can jump 130 times its own height. The record is 33 cm for a long jump and nearly 20 cm for a high jump.

More about: infectious diseases pp24, 30 vaccinations pp14, 30-31

Curing illness

Even a healthy, cared-for animal may become ill sometimes. Mammals catch colds quite easily. This is because there are many 'cold' micro-organisms around, and the body cannot fight them all. The infection may be caught from another animal. Horses can catch colds when they get wet and cold. They must be dried off properly when they are sweating after exercise.

Bacteria, fungi and viruses

Infections are caused by bacteria, fungi or viruses. Bacteria are tiny living things which can be seen only with a microscope. They are all around us, but only some cause disease. Fungi include mushrooms, yeasts and moulds. Some types of fungus live on the skin. Ringworm is a skin condition caused by fungus.

Viruses are even smaller than bacteria. Bacteria are able to multiply very quickly, but viruses cannot multiply unless they are inside the **cells** of bacteria, animals or plants. They invade the cells and infect them. Flu and pneumonia are caused by viruses.

Antibiotics

Illnesses caused by bacteria are usually treated with **antibiotics** if the body cannot fight off the illness. Antibiotics are medicines which kill bacteria or stop them multiplying. Other forms of medicine can be given to ease the **symptoms** of illnesses.

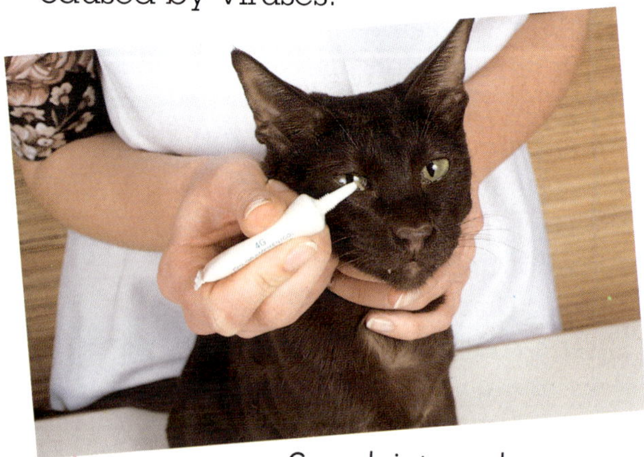

Complaints such as eye, ear and skin infections are often treated with drops or ointments.

Body organs can become diseased. Overweight animals may have a heart attack, so diet and exercise are important. Some animals, such as cats, exercise themselves but dogs have to be taken for walks regularly. A liver diseased by infections or poisons can lead to **jaundice** or **hepatitis**. The liver usually recovers if the cause of disease is removed.

Small animals such as rabbits, hamsters and guinea pigs can become ill because their cages are not cleaned regularly enough. If droppings are left in the cage, they attract flies which spread micro-organisms. Fly strike is a common illness in rabbits.

Animals also have accidents or fight with one another. Wounds have to be dressed to avoid infections. Bones may be broken in an accident. They have to be set in plaster until they mend.

More about: bacteria pp25, 35 infection pp25, 30 liver pp51

Continuing the line

Some people keep animals for **breeding**. When a female is 'in season' or 'on heat', she is ready to mate. If she is allowed to, she will mate with any male she meets. If babies are born, they will be mongrels.

If a Labrador dog mates with another type of dog such as an Alsatian, the puppies will be neither Labradors nor Alsatians, but a mixture of the two.

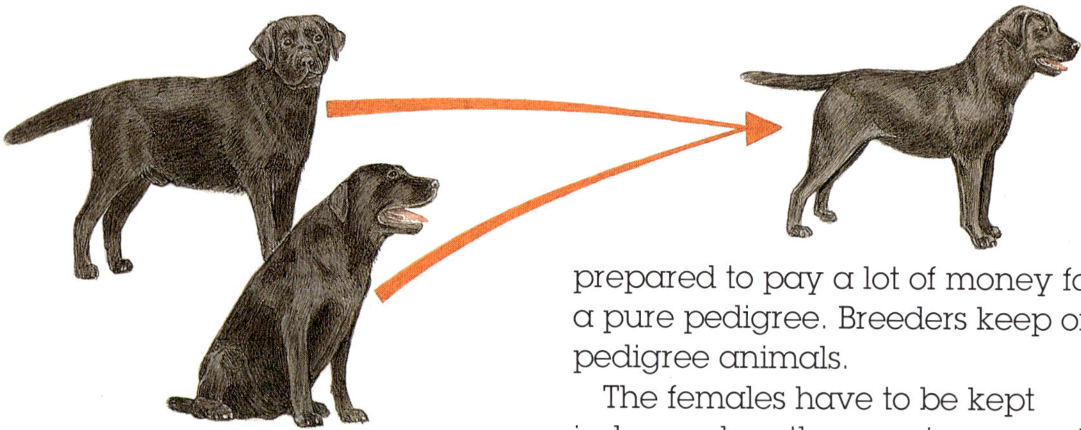

When a female pedigree Labrador mates with a male pedigree Labrador, the puppies will be pure pedigree Labradors.

Pedigree animals

Many people who keep pets are quite happy with a mongrel, but some people want a **pedigree** animal. This means an animal that is bred specially. People are prepared to pay a lot of money for a pure pedigree. Breeders keep only pedigree animals.

The females have to be kept indoors when they are in season to make sure that they do not mate with dogs of another type.

Other pedigree animals, such as cats and horses, are bred in the same way as pedigree dogs. A mare is taken to a stud farm. Here she is mated with a stallion which has all the characteristics that the breeder wants in a new foal. For example, a racehorse must have a slim body that is capable of speed.

Breeders can also produce new varieties by deliberately breeding pedigree animals of different types. The first Burmese cats were produced in 1930 by mating a species of small brown cat from Burma with a Siamese cat.

How animals reproduce

Most mammals reproduce in the same way.

1 Sperm are produced in the male's testes and leave the body through the penis.

2 The female's eggs are produced in the ovaries.

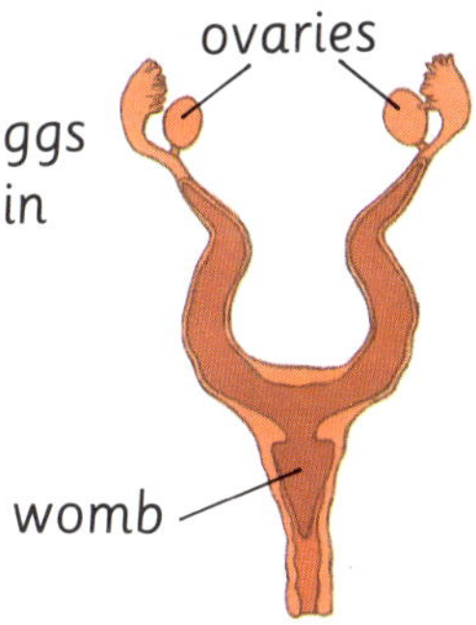

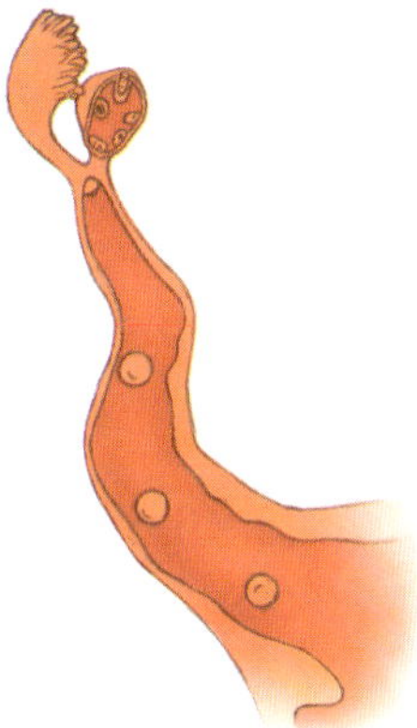

3 When an egg is produced, it passes down to the womb.

4 During mating, the male puts his penis into the female and passes sperm into her body. The sperm are in a liquid and they are far too tiny to see, except with a microscope.

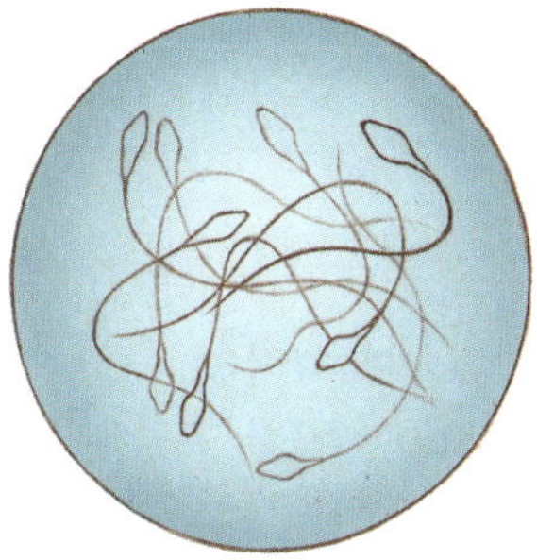

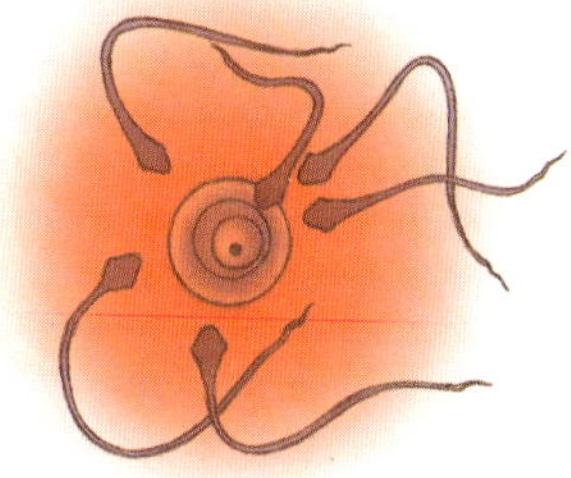

5 The sperm swim towards the egg. If a sperm joins with an egg, the egg is **fertilised**.

6 A baby develops from this egg.

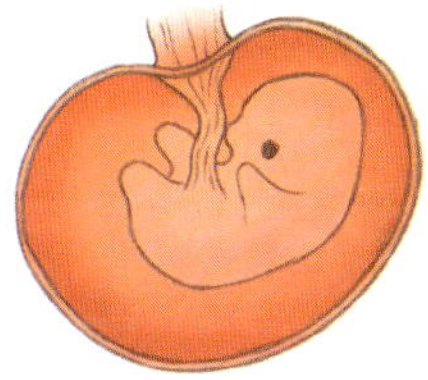

Preventing unwanted babies

If people do not want their animals to breed, they usually decide to have them neutered so that they cannot reproduce. This is a simple operation carried out by the vet. It is called neutering for a male, and spaying for a female.

Did you know...?

The world's smallest horse is the Falabella of Argentina. It was developed over 70 years by breeding a group of very small horses found in southern Argentina. The Falabella is less than 76 cm high.

More about: breeding pp23 operation pp17, 48-49

A day in the life of a vet

1

A vet works in a surgery where people can bring their pets. They telephone the receptionist to make an appointment.

2

This puppy has been brought in to start its course of vaccinations. The vet fills in a chart showing which vaccinations the puppy has had.

3

This gerbil's owner is not sure if his pet is all right. He asks the vet how to look after the gerbil properly.

4

This dog has been in a fight and has a wound on its face. The vet treats the wound. The dog must wear an Elizabethan collar so that it cannot scratch the wound. Deep wounds which are bleeding badly may need stitches. The vet has to sew the edges of the wound together to help it to heal.

5

Emergency! A dog has a bone stuck in its throat. The vet has to remove it before the dogs chokes. Never give dogs bones which splinter, or small objects which can stick in their throats.

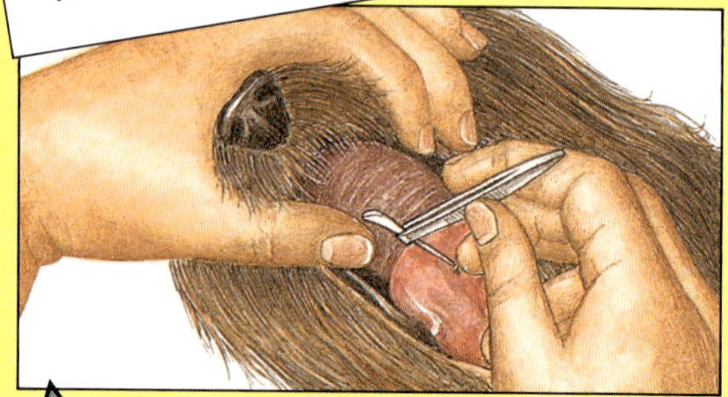

6

After morning surgery it is time for the operations. These operations are usually straightforward. The animal is well enough to go home shortly afterwards. More serious operations are performed in a veterinary hospital.

7

After lunch, the vet sets out on her calls. She has been called to a stables where a horse has colic. This is a build-up of gas in its stomach. The horse is in pain and is not eating properly. The vet gives the horse medicine which gets rid of gas.

8

The vet visits a farm where a cow is expecting a calf. The calf is not facing in the right direction for birth. The vet has to turn it inside the cow.

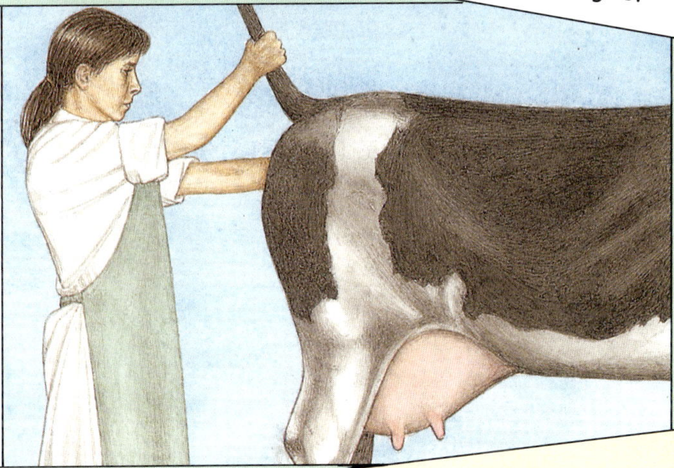

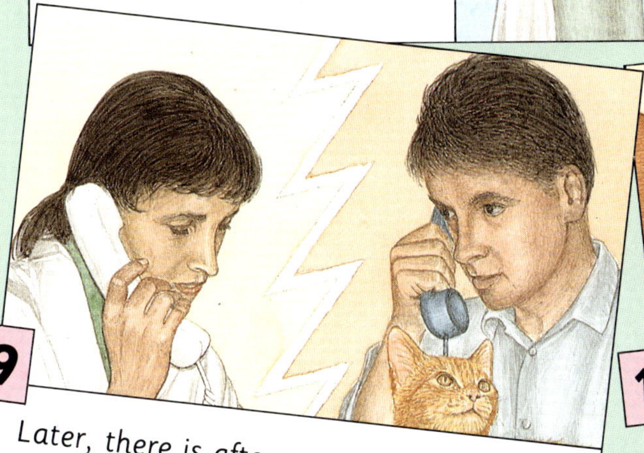

9

Later, there is afternoon surgery. People also phone for advice if their pet seems unwell.

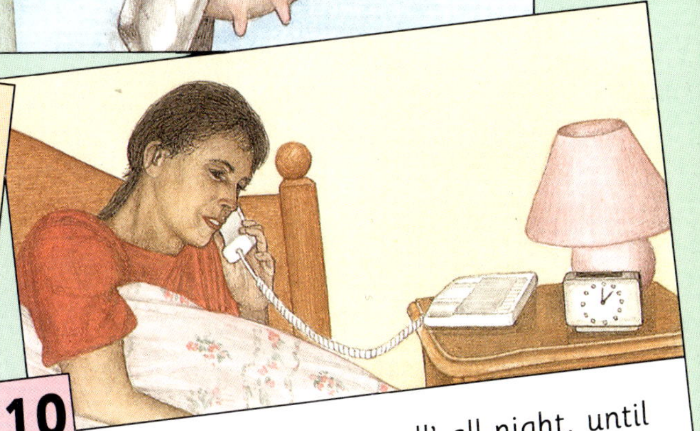

10

One of the vets is 'on call' all night, until surgery starts the next morning. She is available for any emergencies or accidents that happen during the night.

More about: vaccination pp8, 30-31 veterinary hospital pp16-17

Into hospital

An animal with a serious illness or broken bones may have to go to a veterinary hospital for treatment. Veterinary hospitals are run in the same way as hospitals for humans. Hospital vets specialise in different types of treatment. The hospital has nurses to look after the animals as they recover. Vets and animal nurses have a similar training to the doctors and nurses who work in hospitals.

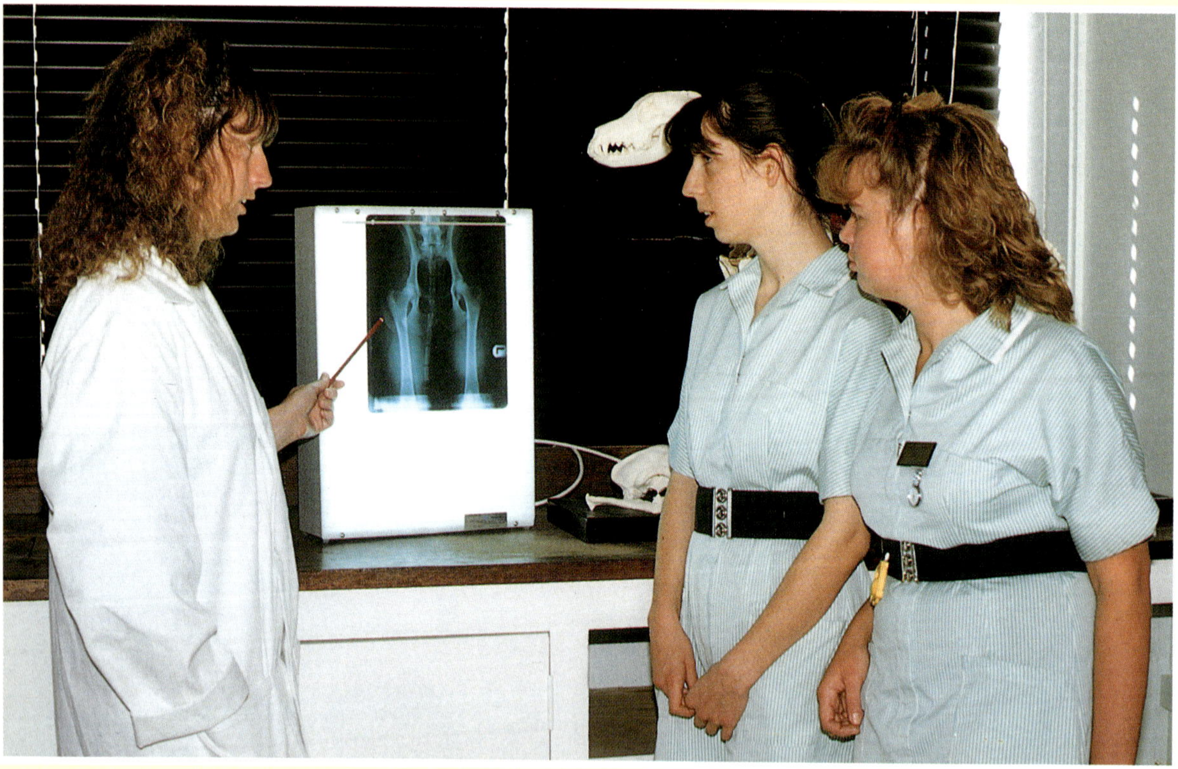

*A **radiographer** takes an X-ray of the injured part of an animal so the vets can see whether any bones are broken. An X-ray also shows where a break is.*

Hospital departments

The hospital is divided into different departments. For example, if an animal has been injured in a road accident, it is first taken to the X-ray department.

The animal is taken to the **orthopaedic** department to have the bones set. The orthopaedic department deals with any disorders of the bones or joints. Broken bones are set in plaster until they mend.

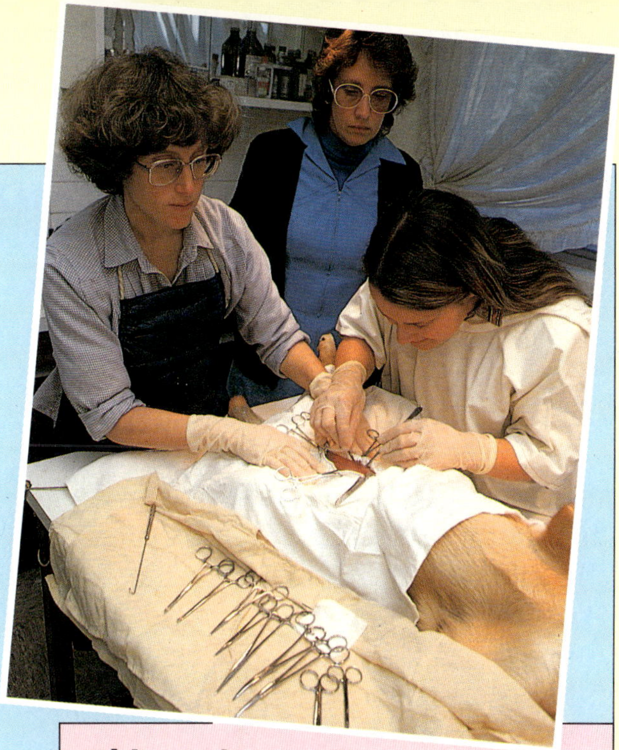

Operations

Operations are carried out in the operating theatre. First, an **anaesthetist** puts the animal to sleep so that it does not feel any pain and keeps still during the operation. The **anaesthetic** is usually given by injection.

Operations include repairing damaged organs and removing 'foreign bodies' which the animal may have swallowed. Horses with severe colic may need an operation to remove blockages in the **digestive system**.

Did you know...?

In the USA, there are special hospitals for reptiles such as snakes and iguanas. Some animal hospitals in the UK now have special departments for reptiles.

There is also a dental department to deal with problems with the teeth.

Nursing animals

Animals are nursed until they are well enough to go home. Vets and nurses are on duty night and day. They give medicines regularly, take temperatures and check that the animals are eating properly.

Animals with broken bones must exercise once the bones have healed. This strengthens the muscles around the bones. Sometimes heavy animals such as horses are put into a swimming pool to exercise. The water supports the weight of the animal's body.

More about: exercise pp47, 54-55 X-rays pp33, 44-45

At an animal centre

Sometimes people find animals that are injured, ill or have been abandoned by their owners. What can be done?

In Britain, organisations such as the Royal Society for the Prevention of Cruelty to Animals (RSPCA) and the International League for the Protection of Horses (ILPH) run animal centres which look after injured or stray animals. There are also private animal sanctuaries. These take in wild or domesticated animals in need of help or treatment. The animals may be starving and in poor condition.

Animal centres

Many of the animals taken in are pets which have lost their home. Sometimes the owners cannot look after the animal any more and they ask the centre to find it a new home. Most are dogs and cats, but centres also take small animals such as rabbits and guinea pigs.

Some large animal centres have a resident vet, but the smaller ones call in the local vet if an animal needs treatment.

This is how one Exmoor pony looked when she came to the ILPH.

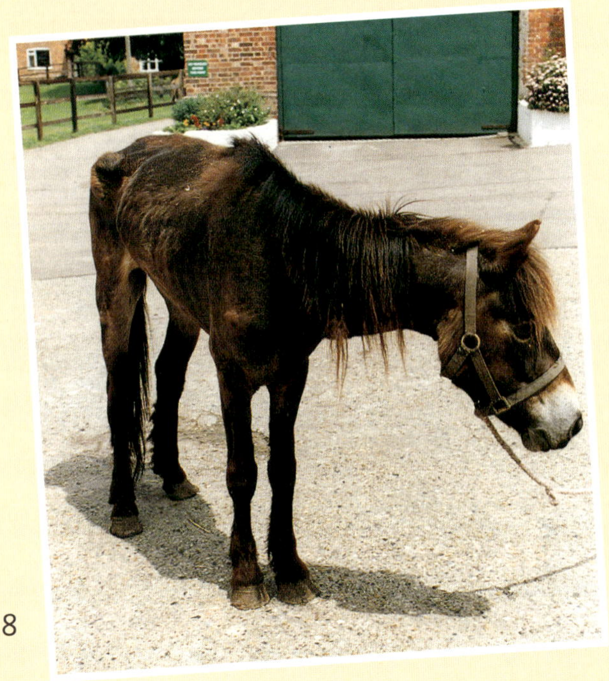

This is how the same pony looked 6 months later. What differences can you see in the pony?

Wildlife sanctuaries

Wild animals sometimes need treatment. They might have been injured in an accident. People find birds with broken wings. Baby animals may have been deserted by their mother before they are old enough to look after themselves. Wild animals can be taken to a special wildlife sanctuary or hospital.

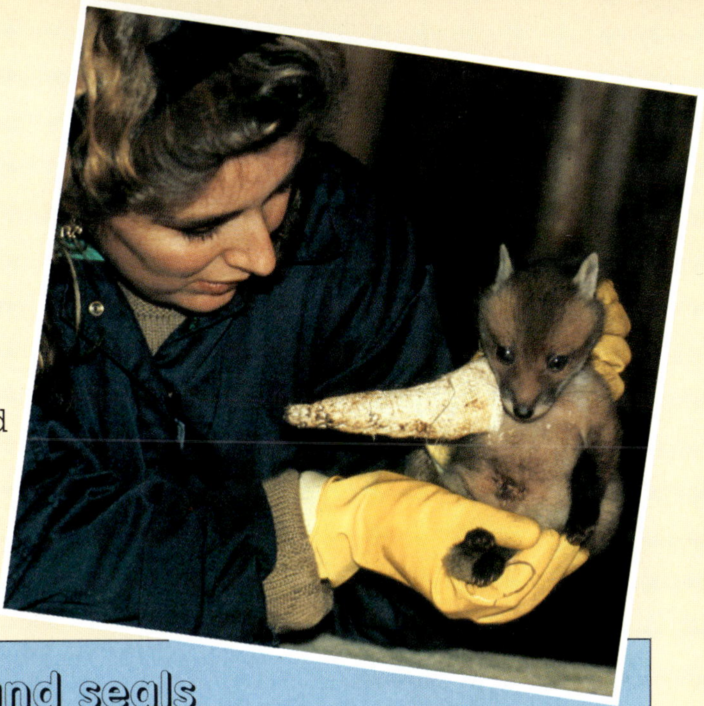

Treating oiled birds and seals

If there is a disaster such as an oil spillage at sea, many animals may be killed by the **pollution**. Sea birds become coated with oil. Seals, fish and other animals are poisoned if they swallow oil.

Some wildlife centres have special units for treating oiled birds. The birds have to be cleaned thoroughly. They are then kept at the centre for a few days until their feathers have become waterproof again.

Sometimes sick or injured seals are found. They may be suffering from poisoning or some other illness. They can be taken to a seal sanctuary for treatment. If the seals are cured, they are released back into the sea.

A bird's feathers keep out the cold and wet. They cannot do this if they are stuck together with oil. The bird will die from cold if it is not treated quickly.

More about: broken bones pp16 poisoning pp34-35

At the zoo

Today, many zoo animals are born in captivity. If they are moved around, it is usually from one zoo to another. But they are still wild animals. Their natural **habitats** vary from the tropical rain forest to the Arctic seas. The animals should be looked after properly. They must be kept in conditions which match their natural **environment**. Otherwise, they may become ill.

New arrivals

Problems can arise when a new animal arrives at a zoo. Being moved is unsettling for the animal. It might also be carrying a disease which it could pass on to other animals.

In the UK, all animals arriving from overseas have to go into **quarantine** for six months. This means that they are kept apart from other animals. They are then watched carefully to make sure that they do not show any signs of disease.

A large zoo has its own quarantine station. After six months, the animals are transferred to cages, tanks, or open areas with other animals.

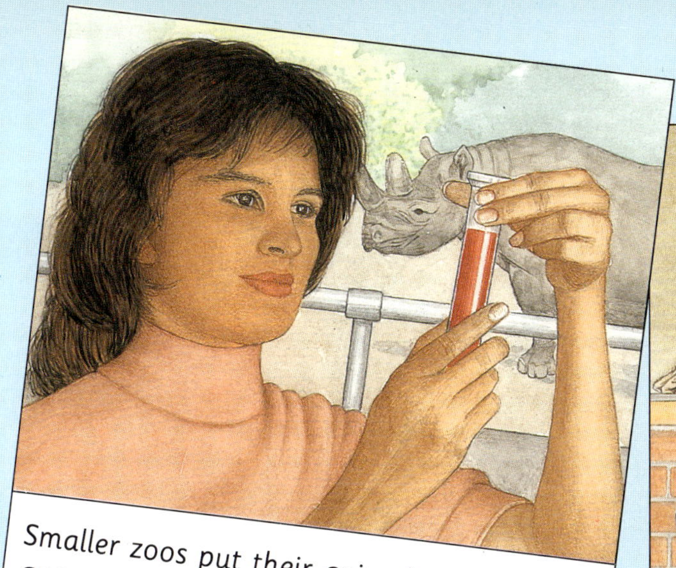

Smaller zoos put their animals in quarantine elsewhere. A new animal is kept on its own for about a week after quarantine. Keepers check the animal's health and take blood samples.

Zoo animals need worming just as pets do. Keepers worm a single animal by crushing a tablet in its food.

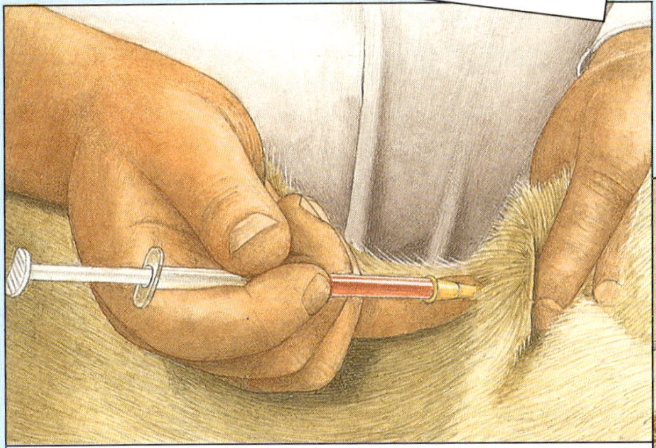

When animals are in a group, the keeper usually catches each animal in turn. The animal is given an injection to worm it.

A new arrival from the wild may be unwell because of **stress**. It may be less resistant to bacteria. It would probably be given a course of antibiotics to kill off any bacteria.

Did you know...?

There are about 760 zoos in the world and more than 350 million people visit them each year.

More about: bacteria pp4, 10, 25, 35 injection pp8, 31, 48 worming pp9

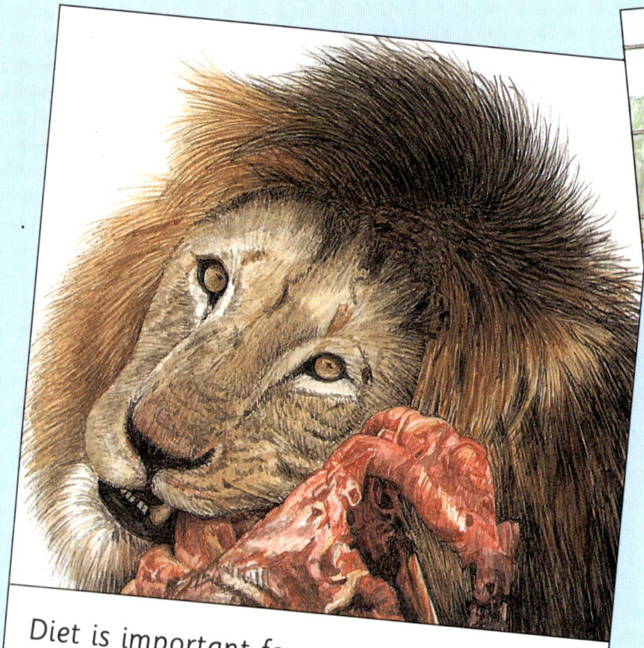

Diet is important for zoo animals as well. They have to be given the type of food that they are used to eating in the wild. Meat-eaters such as lions eat large amounts of raw meat...

... the **primates** such as apes and monkeys eat fruit...

... seals and sea lions eat fish. The animals have special feeding times each day when their keeper brings them their food.

The keepers also clean out the animals' cages regularly. This contact helps the keepers to monitor the animals from day to day.

Did you know...?

The earliest known collection of animals was set up by Shulgi, a ruler of Ur in Mesopotamia from 2097–2094 BC.

Calling the vet

If an animal is sick and the keeper is not sure what is wrong, he or she contacts the vet. Large zoos may have a resident vet. Smaller zoos call in the local vet who comes to see the animal. The keeper usually treats the animal, under instruction from the vet.

Why have zoos?

Zoos have an important role to play. In the wild, many animals are becoming **extinct** because of hunting, the clearance of forests and other interference by people. Animals in zoos are protected. They are helped to breed in captivity and so continue the species.

However, the zoo has to be properly managed. If an animal is not happy, it will stop breeding. The environment of the zoo has to match the animal's natural environment as closely as possible. Animals kept in cramped cages suffer stress and cannot move around as they do in the wild. Animals should be given as much space as possible so they can exercise.

More about: breeding pp12-13 diet pp29, 54-55 stress pp21, 53, 55

Going to the doctor

When you are ill you go to the doctor. A doctor has to train for at least five years to learn all about the body, how it works and what can go wrong with it.

Everyone should be registered with a doctor so that they can be seen quickly if they are ill. Your 'family doctor' is called a **general practitioner** or GP. A GP works at a surgery, usually with a partner or group of other doctors. Most people register with a GP who has a surgery close to where they live.

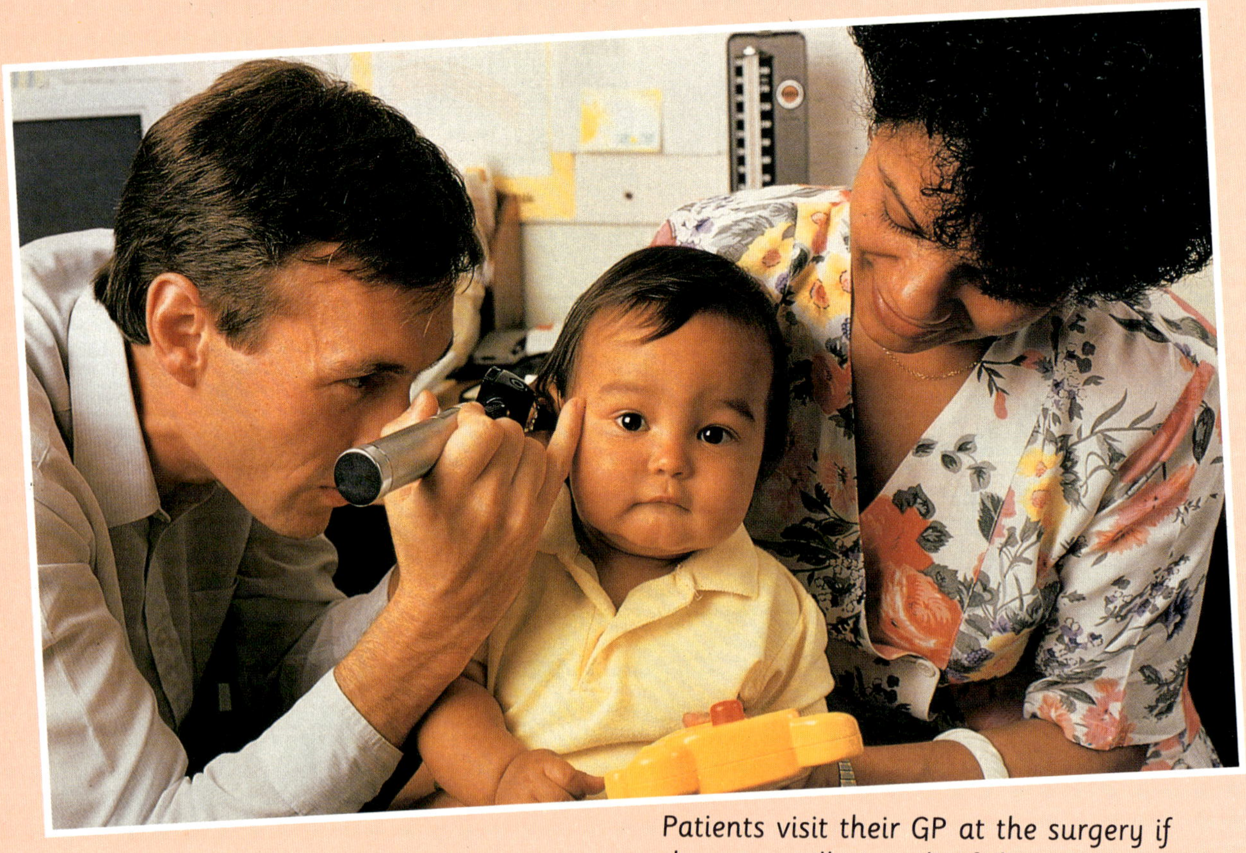

Patients visit their GP at the surgery if they are well enough. If they are very ill, the doctor visits them at home.

What sort of illness?

First, the doctor has to decide what sort of illness the patient has.

Some infectious illnesses can be passed on through micro-organisms which breed in dirty water or unhygienic conditions. Infectious and contagious illnesses are caused by bacteria, viruses and fungi, just as they are in animals.

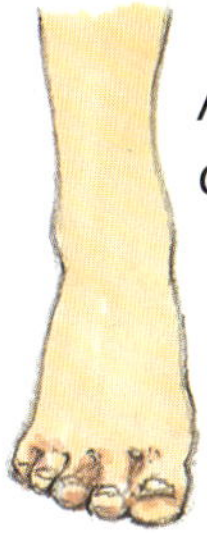

Athlete's foot is caused by a fungus.

Pneumonia is caused by bacteria.

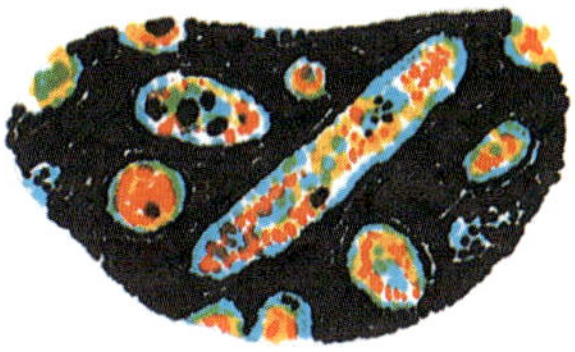

Most common illnesses are caused by infections. Some infectious illnesses are **contagious**. They are passed on by contact with other people, such as through touch. Some illnesses are passed on by breathing in micro-organisms.

Colds and flu are caused by viruses.

Some disorders are **genetic**. This means that a baby inherits the illness from its parents through their **genes**.

Staying healthy

You will help your body to resist illness if you follow a healthy lifestyle. Smoking cigarettes and drinking too much alcohol damages the body. Make sure you relax and get enough sleep. Take plenty of exercise. Eat healthy foods such as fruit and vegetables. Say 'No' to too many fatty and starchy foods such as hamburgers, chips and cakes. Choose wholemeal bread instead of white bread.

More about: bacteria pp4, 10, 35 genes pp26 viruses pp10, 30

Genetic illness

Some people are born with an illness which has been passed on from a parent. Sometimes the illness is not noticeable at birth and the symptoms develop later in life.

Genes

A baby starts life as an egg (from the woman) which has been fertilised by a sperm (from the man). The egg and the sperm both contain genes. Genes are sets of instructions about what the baby will **inherit** from its parents. This includes illnesses which 'run in the family'.

Skipping a generation

A baby does not always inherit family illnesses. Sometimes genetic illnesses 'skip a generation'; a grandparent has it, the parent does not, but the baby does. Sometimes one child has the illness, but brothers and sisters do not. It depends on the exact set of instructions passed on from each egg and sperm.

Find out more about genes in the *New Horizons* book, *Look you! Look me!*

Asthma, eczema, and hay fever are genetic conditions. Migraine and some heart conditions also tend to run in families.

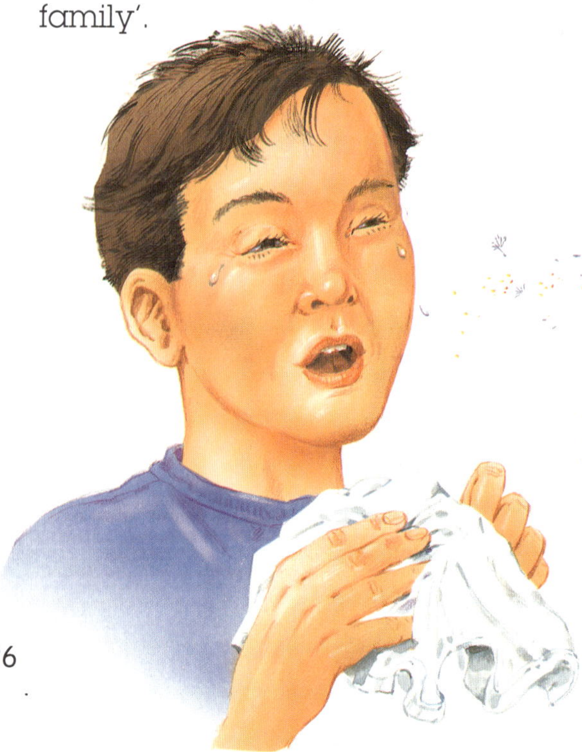

Hay fever is an ***allergy****. Sufferers are allergic to the pollen from plants. It makes them cough, sneeze and have painful, streaming eyes.*

Haemophilia

Haemophilia is a hereditary bleeding disorder. When you cut yourself, your blood **clots** and forms a scab to stop the bleeding. A haemophiliac's blood does not clot, so the wound carries on bleeding. All haemophiliacs are male, but women are carriers of the condition. This means that women do not actually suffer from the disorder themselves, but may pass it on to their sons.

Haemophilia used to be a fatal illness. Now it can be controlled by giving the haemophiliac blood from a person who is not a sufferer. This helps the blood to clot. Giving a person blood from someone else is known as a **blood transfusion**.

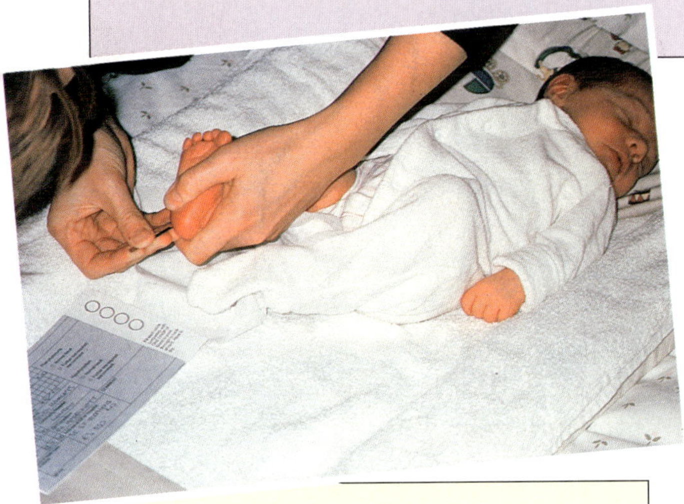

People who are worried about a hereditary illness can have regular check-ups by their doctor. Babies are checked soon after birth. This is known as screening. In this case the midwife is taking a blood sample from the baby's heel. The blood will then be tested.

Did you know...?

Colour blindness is an inherited condition. Most people who are colour blind cannot tell the difference between certain colours, such as red and green. Truly colour blind people see everything in black, white and grey. This is very rare. About 7·5 % of men and 0·1 % of women are colour blind.

The average human, using both eyes in good condition, can see 10 million different shades of colour.

Try these tests for colour blindness. What can you see?

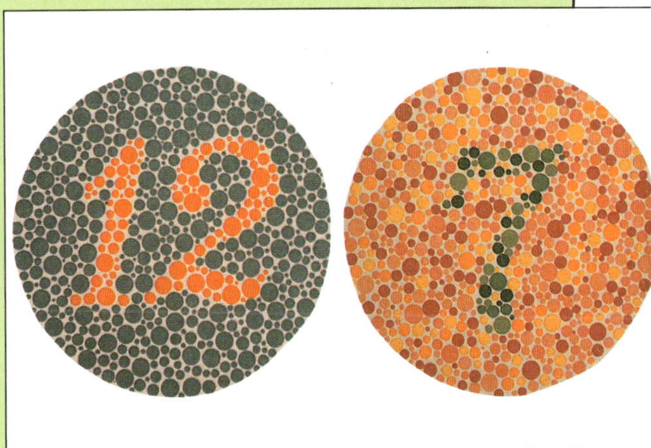

More about: blood pp32-33, 58-59 heart conditions pp52-53

Illnesses caused by parasites

Parasites live in or on the body of animals, including humans. They feed on blood or tissue. Some parasites can cause disease.

Malaria

Malaria is a serious disease which is spread by a certain type of mosquito. Mosquitoes spread malarial parasites which are known as *Plasmodia*. When the mosquito bites, the parasite is injected into the blood. It multiplies in the red blood cells and begins to spread through the body. The first symptoms of malaria are shaking, chills and a fever. The patient has to be treated with anti-malarial drugs for several weeks.

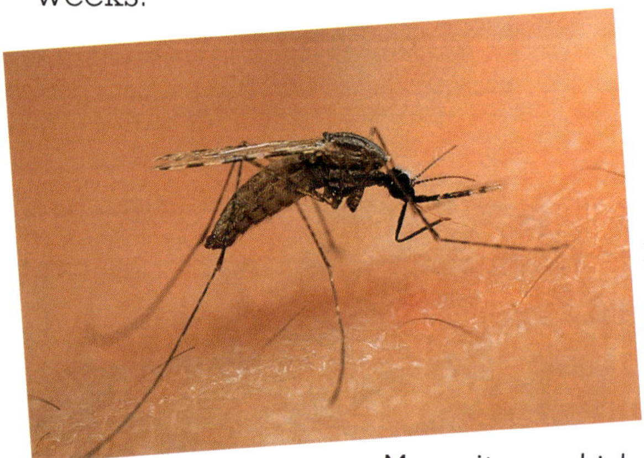

Mosquitoes which spread malaria are found throughout the tropics, where malaria is very common. The disease affects about 300 million people in the world each year.

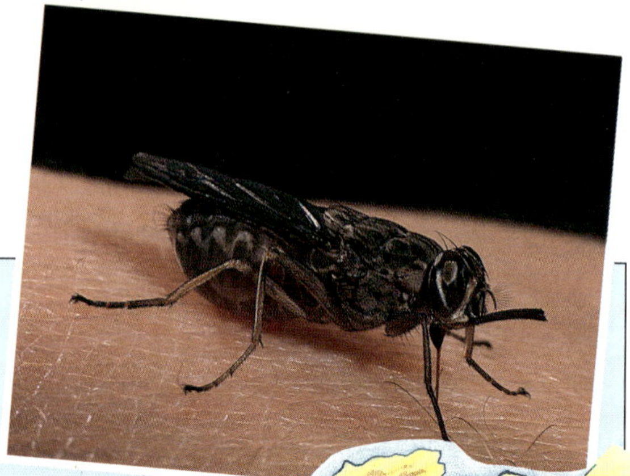

tsetse fly

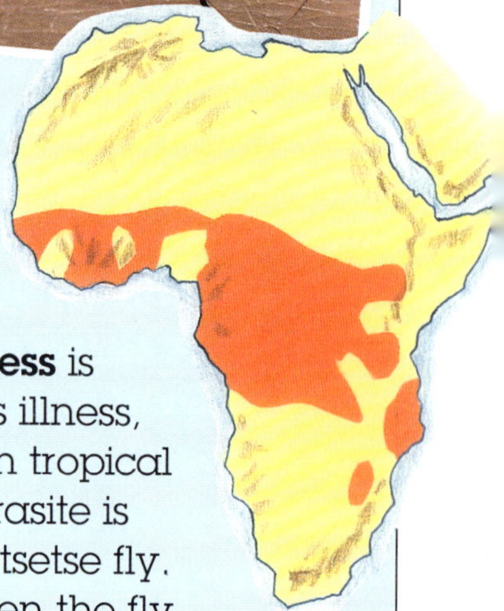

Sleeping sickness

Sleeping sickness is another serious illness, which occurs in tropical Africa. The parasite is carried by the tsetse fly. It is spread when the fly bites a person or animal. Sleeping sickness affects the nervous system. If it is not treated quickly, it can spread to the heart and then the brain. The disease can be fatal, but most cases are completely cured with drugs.

Malaria can be a fatal disease. Every year, it kills about 1 million babies and children in Africa alone. It is the most dangerous disease for travellers to tropical areas. However, it can be prevented by taking anti-malarial drugs.

Illnesses caused by diet

A balanced diet is very important for a healthy body. A lack of certain **nutrients** can cause illness. Children may develop **rickets** if they do not have enough vitamin D. The bones become deformed as the child grows. The legs look bowed and in babies, the skull softens and looks flatter. Sometimes the bones of the wrists and ankles get bigger .

Iron is a mineral which is essential for the production of haemoglobin. Liver, lean meat, eggs, wholemeal bread and green vegetables are good sources of iron.

Rickets is treated by taking vitamin D. Oily fish, butter, eggs, liver and milk are good sources of vitamin D.

The red cells in your blood carry oxygen round the body in a substance called haemoglobin. Sometimes the number of red cells is reduced, or there is not enough haemoglobin in the cells. This leads to a disorder called **anaemia**. The most common type of anaemia is caused by a lack of iron. People with anaemia feel tired and have headaches. The skin may look pale.

Did you know...?

In the 15th and 16th centuries, sailors on long voyages often died from scurvy. Scurvy is a skin disease caused by a lack of vitamin C. Captain Cook managed to prevent his crew getting scurvy on his voyage to Australia in 1768. He made his crew eat citrus fruit, which are rich in vitamin C, and took plenty of fresh food on board during the voyage.

Find out more about diet in the *New Horizons* book, *Look you! Look me!*

More about: blood pp32-33, 58-59 brain pp51 heart pp50, 52-53

Other illnesses

Flu and the common cold are two illnesses caused by viruses. They are contagious. Many people suffer from both of them each year, particularly in winter.

Viruses are difficult to treat because there are hundreds of different types. If you have a cold, the best thing to do is rest, keep warm, take medicines such as aspirin and wait until it goes away. Measles and whooping cough, and even more serious illnesses such as typhoid and smallpox, can be prevented by vaccination.

Bronchitis is an infection of the **bronchii**, the airways that connect the windpipe to the lungs. It sometimes develops after a bad cold or flu. Pneumonia is an infection of the lungs.

Chicken pox and mumps are also caused by viruses. They are known as 'childhood illnesses' because children tend to catch them and pass them to each other. They can be serious for adults who catch them.

Did you know...?

The longest sneezing fit on record lasted 977 days.

Polio

Some infectious illnesses are very serious. Polio, which is short for *poliomyelitis*, is an infectious disease caused by a virus.

Sometimes, the infected person recovers completely. But the virus can attack the brain and nerves in the spine. This may lead to permanent **paralysis** (loss of movement), or to death.
It is still serious in some parts of the world, particularly in poorer countries, which cannot afford to have everyone vaccinated.

The first vaccination

In 1980, the World Health Organisation stated that smallpox no longer existed throughout the world, because of successful vaccination.

1 Smallpox is a highly infectious disease which was common in the 19th century and before. It is caused by a virus. A person developed a rash which spread all over the body. The rash then developed into blisters. The blisters often left deep scars. Nearly half of all smallpox sufferers died.

2 In 1796, Edward Jenner noticed that milkmaids often got a rash called cowpox from the cows they milked. But they never caught smallpox.

3 Jenner realised that cowpox made people **immune** to smallpox. He experimented by infecting a boy with some cowpox bacteria.

4 The boy caught cowpox, but soon recovered. Then Jenner infected him with smallpox in the same way. The boy remained healthy.

5 This was the first vaccination. The same method is now used to protect people from many diseases.

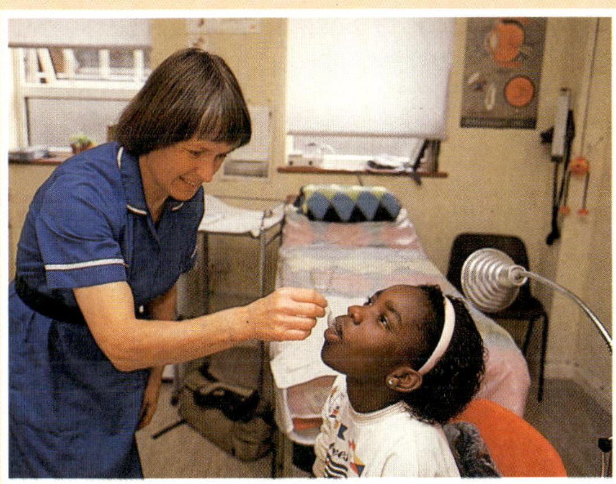

Children are now vaccinated against polio. In the UK this was started in 1956. Since then, the number of cases has dropped from several thousand a year to three or four.

Did you know...?

The word vaccination comes from the Latin vacca which means 'cow'.

More about: colds pp25 vaccination pp8, 14 viruses pp10, 25

Diagnosing an illness

If you have a sore throat and a bad cough, the doctor will ask some questions about your cough.

Then your temperature is taken. Your mouth is checked in case of any infection or swelling in your throat. The doctor also listens to your chest with a **stethoscope**.

Other checks can be carried out to diagnose an illness. The **pulse** in the wrist allows the doctor to feel the heartbeat. The pulse beats as blood is pumped through the **artery** by the heart. The doctor takes the patient's pulse by putting two fingers over the main artery in the wrist and counting the pulse beats.

A stethoscope **amplifies** sounds in the heart and lungs. As you breathe in and out, the doctor can hear what is going on inside.

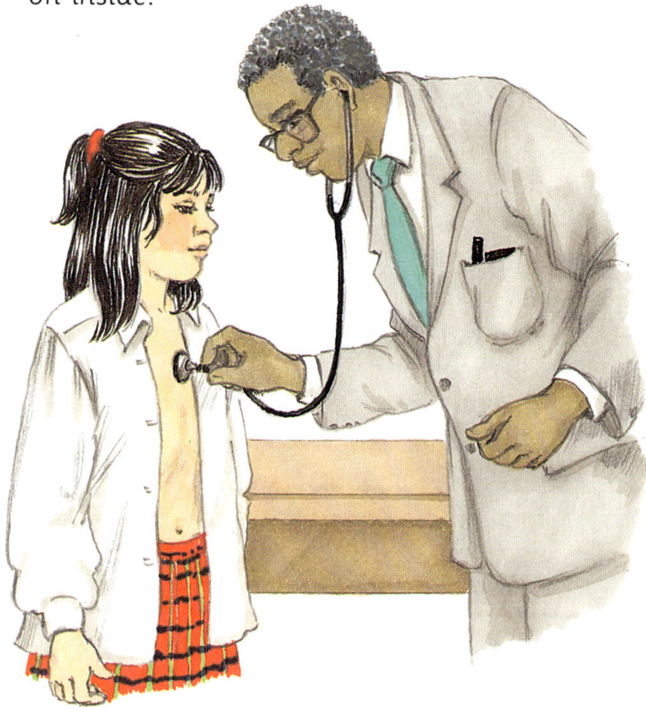

Blood pressure

Blood pressure is the force with which your heart pumps blood around your body. High blood pressure puts a strain on the heart. Blood pressure may be too high if a person is overweight, for example. Very low blood pressure prevents the flow of blood to the brain and leads to dizziness and fainting.

Hospital diagnoses

A GP can carry out only a general examination at the surgery. If patients need an X-ray or a special examination, the GP sends them to hospital to be diagnosed.

What instruments have you seen a doctor use? What does he or she use to examine your ears and eyes?

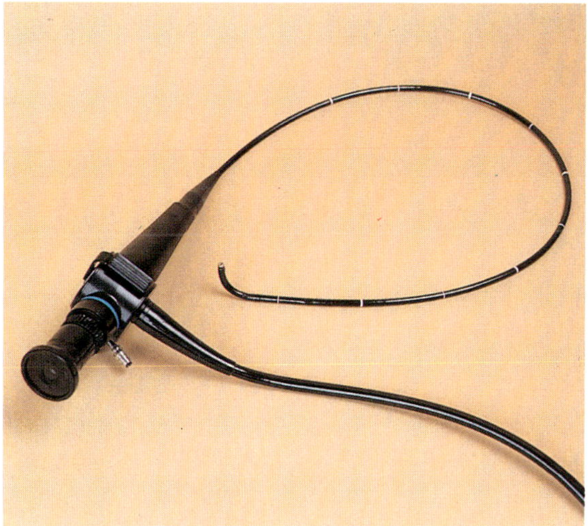

An **endoscope** is a ***fibre optic*** instrument for looking inside the body. It contains a bundle of thin glass fibres which reflect light. The fibres bend as the doctor guides the endoscope into the body. The doctor looks through a magnifying lens at the top.

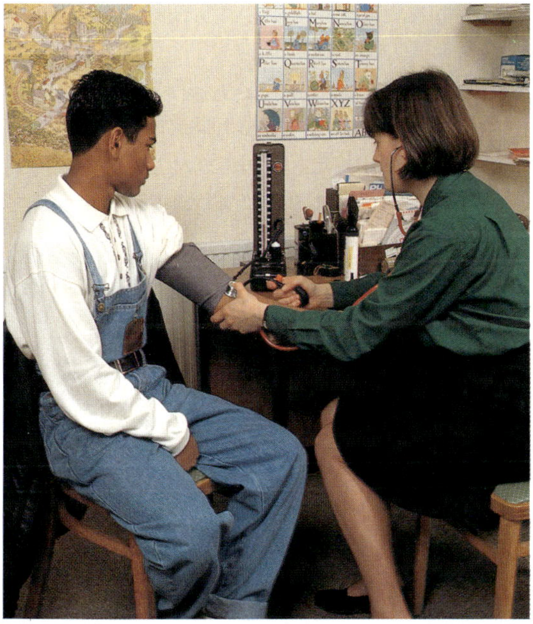

The doctor measures blood pressure with a special instrument. A cuff is wrapped round the arm and inflated until it stops the blood supply. The doctor then listens to the blood pumping as the cuff is deflated.

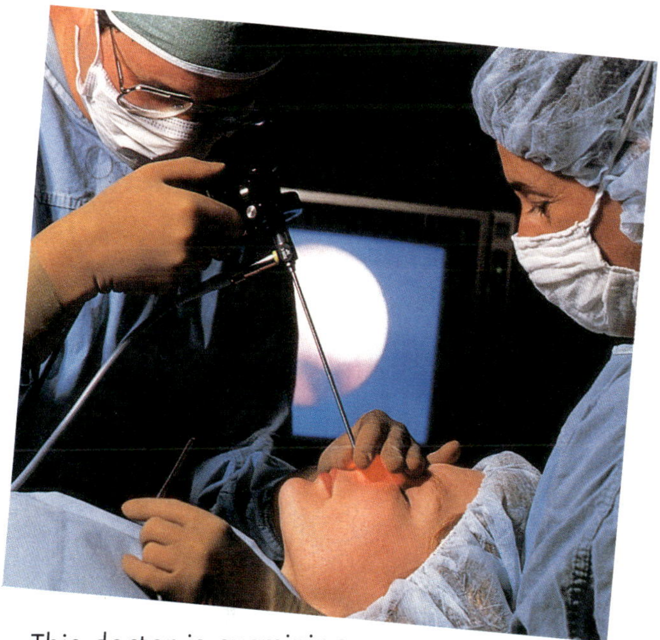

This doctor is examining the inside of the nose using an endoscope.

More about: blood pp27, 58-59 hospital pp16-17, 44-45 X-ray pp16, 44-45

Food poisoning

Food poisoning is quite separate from other illnesses. It strikes very suddenly. It is caused by eating food which has been **contaminated** by bacteria or viruses.

Someone with food poisoning has bad stomach pains and is very sick. This is the body's way of getting rid of the contaminated food. (Stomach pains and sickness can be the symptoms of other illnesses as well.) A doctor would normally suspect food poisoning if a person has been well until eating a meal, or if a group of people who have eaten the same food are all taken ill.

How is food contaminated?

Food can be contaminated in different ways. Most cases of food poisoning are caused by bad hygiene. Food should always be thoroughly cooked to kill bacteria.

Dirty kitchens and food that is going bad are breeding grounds for bacteria.

Frozen food should be thawed out completely, otherwise bacteria may not be killed when the food is cooked.

What can you see here that could cause food poisoning?

Shellfish such as mussels and oysters can be contaminated by bacteria or viruses. This happens if they eat poisonous ***plankton****, or if they live in polluted water.*

One group of bacteria which causes food poisoning is *Salmonella*. Someone with *Salmonella* poisoning has stomach pains, sickness, headaches and sometimes shivering and fever. In most cases, the symptoms last only two or three days. The patient has to replace lost fluids by drinking a lot of water.

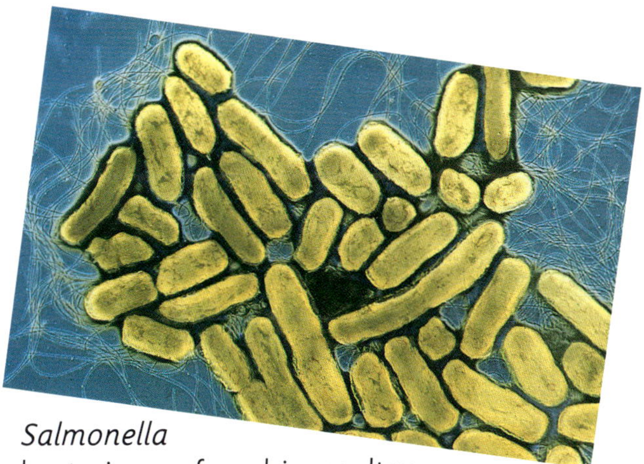

Salmonella bacteria are found in poultry products such as hens' eggs and chicken. Salmonella poisoning can be avoided by cooking eggs and chicken properly so that any bacteria are killed.

Botulism

Botulism is a rare but very serious type of food poisoning. It comes from eating canned or **preserved** food which has been contaminated with botulism bacteria. The bacteria can survive boiling, salting, smoking and some types of pickling. Someone with botulism must be treated with an **antitoxin** as soon as possible. An antitoxin stops the action of the poison.

Some foods go bad quickly in hot conditions such as in a car left in the sun. Always pack picnics at the last minute and put food in airtight containers. Store the picnic in a cool place in the car, out of direct sunlight.

More about: bacteria pp10, 25 poisoning pp19 pollution pp19

Treating illness

When an illness has been diagnosed, the doctor has to decide how to treat it. You may be given a **prescription** for medicine or **drugs**.

Antibiotics

Antibiotics are available only with a prescription. Some antibiotics kill bacteria. Others prevent them from multiplying, which gives the body a chance to fight the disease. Some antibiotics work only on certain types of bacteria, while others are effective against a wider range.

Before prescribing antibiotics, doctors ask patients if they are allergic to any type of antibiotics. For example, some people are allergic to penicillin. They get 'side effects' such as sickness and dizziness. This can make them feel worse than the illness they are suffering from!

Analgesics

Some drugs relieve the symptoms of illnesses, but do not kill the micro-organisms which cause them. These are known as **analgesics**. They relieve fever and pain and so are taken for colds, flu and headaches. Aspirin and paracetamol are analgesics which you can buy at a chemist's shop.

Penicillin was the first antibiotic. It was discovered by Alexander Fleming in 1928, and it is still widely used today.

You can buy some drugs over the counter at a chemist's shop. Others can be supplied only with a doctor's prescription. **Pharmacists** often have to prepare the drugs at the chemist's shop.

Drugs can be given in the form of tablets, in a syrup or as injections. Creams and lotions are sometimes prescribed for skin conditions.

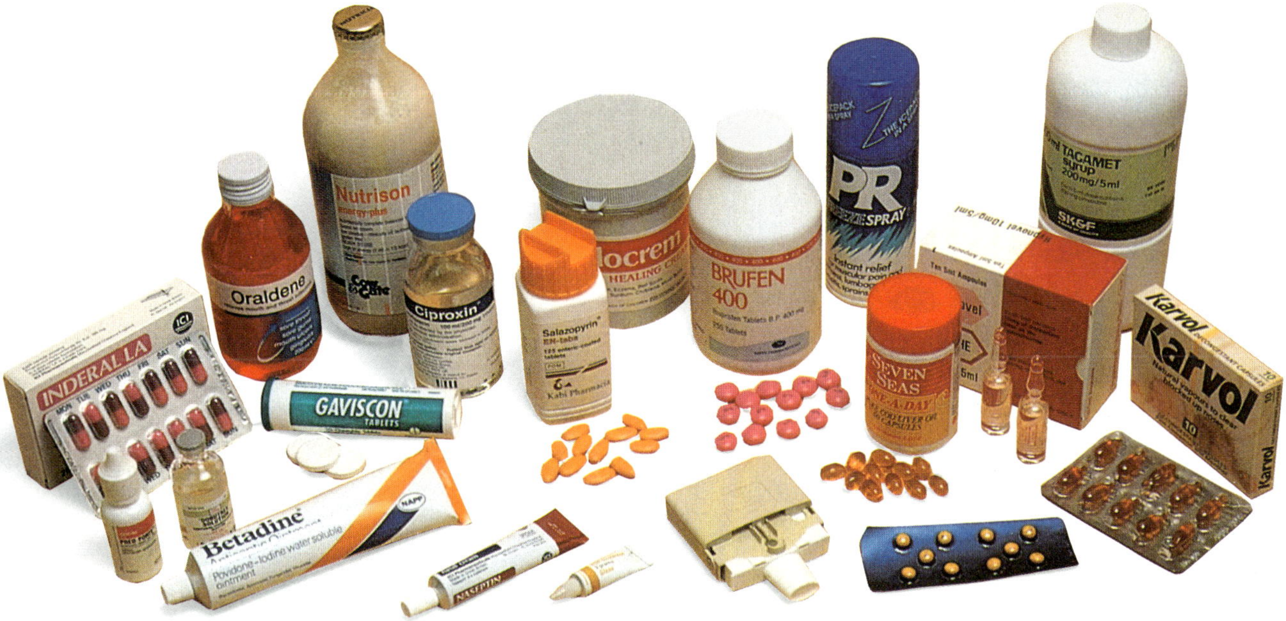

What are drugs made of?

Many plants and herbs have healing properties. People have been using them for centuries. For example, antibiotics can be made from some types of moulds and fungi. Digitalis, which is used to treat heart disease, is found in foxglove leaves. Can you find more examples?

Some plants are poisonous. Always check with an adult before you touch, pick or eat part of a plant.

Did you know...?

The natives of the South American tropical rain forests make medicines from plants. For example, there are at least 2000 plants which can be used in medicines to treat cancer.

More about: drugs pp38-39 fungi pp10, 25 heart disease pp52-53

Drug abuse

Medicines can be dangerous if they are not taken in the right amounts. Taking too many or too much can kill you. Strong drugs are strictly controlled by doctors. The patient cannot get the drug without a prescription.

Even the drugs you can buy from a chemist, such as paracetamol and aspirin, can kill if someone takes an **overdose**.

The doctor writes a prescription for a drug. The prescription says how much of the drug the patient should take each time.

All drugs should be locked away. Small children might think they are sweets. Some household substances, such as bleach, are poisonous. They should also be kept out of reach of small children.

Did you know...?

The largest chain of chemists' stores in the world is Boots The Chemists, founded by Jesse Boot (1850—1931).

Tranquillisers

People can become dependent on prescription drugs such as sleeping pills or **tranquillisers**. Doctors sometimes prescribe tranquillisers, such as valium, for people who are feeling nervy. The tranquillisers do calm them down, but after a while their bodies become used to the drug. They find it difficult to stop taking it.

Drug dependence

Not all drugs are medicines. People take some drugs to feel good or relaxed. As their bodies get used to a drug, they need to take more and more to have the same effect. Soon they cannot do without it. They are then **dependent** on the drug.

Alcohol and the nicotine in cigarettes are drugs to which people can become ***addicted****. Other drugs such as cocaine and heroin are very dangerous. It is against the law to use these drugs in Britain.*

Drug dependence may cause permanent damage to the body. Drinking too much alcohol can damage the liver. Cigarettes can cause lung cancer and heart disease. Taking drugs over a long period gradually poisons the body and damages the organs.

Coming off drugs

People who try to stop taking drugs they are addicted to, often get **withdrawal symptoms**. The body feels a need for the drugs and reacts strongly when it does not get them. Symptoms may include shaking, cramps, sweating and feverishness, and being sick. People who are addicted to drugs sometimes have to stay in a clinic or hospital while they come off the drug gradually. They receive treatment for the withdrawal symptoms at the same time. They may also need **counselling** to deal with the problems which led to taking drugs in the first place.

More about: drugs pp36-37 liver pp51 poison pp19

A day in the life of a GP

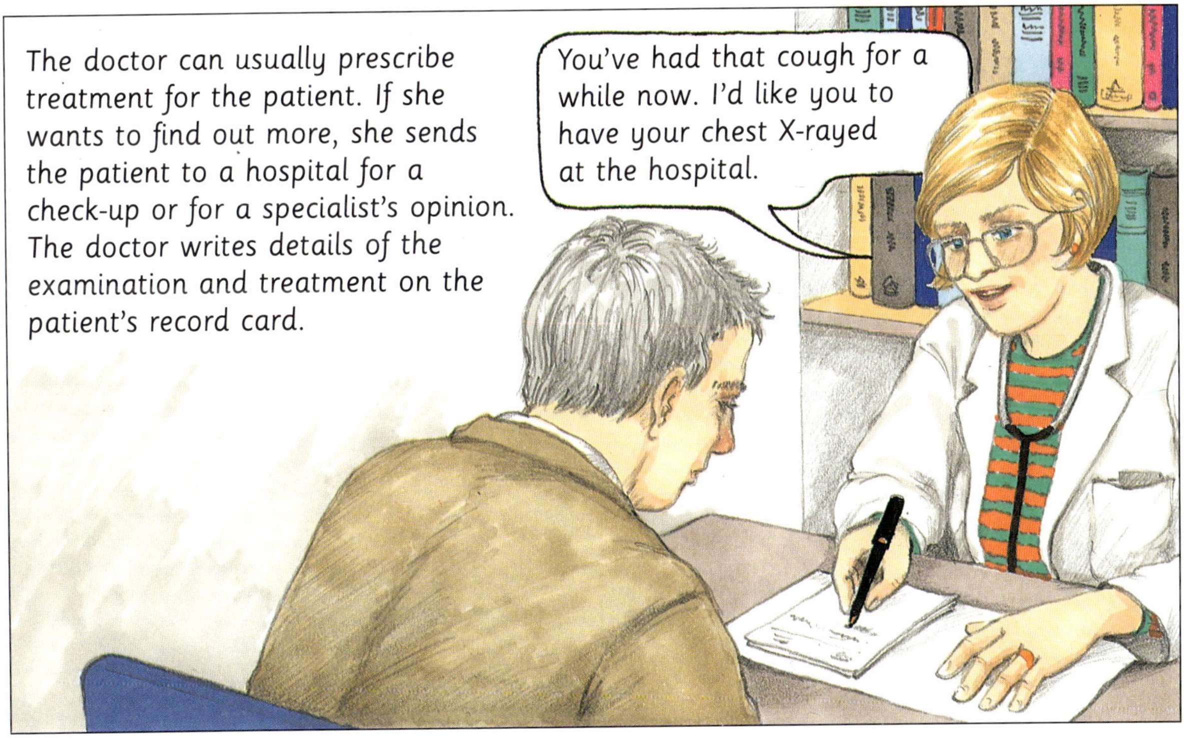

More about: allergy pp26 hospital pp16-17, 44-45 prescription pp36, 38

There is a nurse at the surgery to give injections and change dressings. A midwife visits to examine women who are expecting babies.

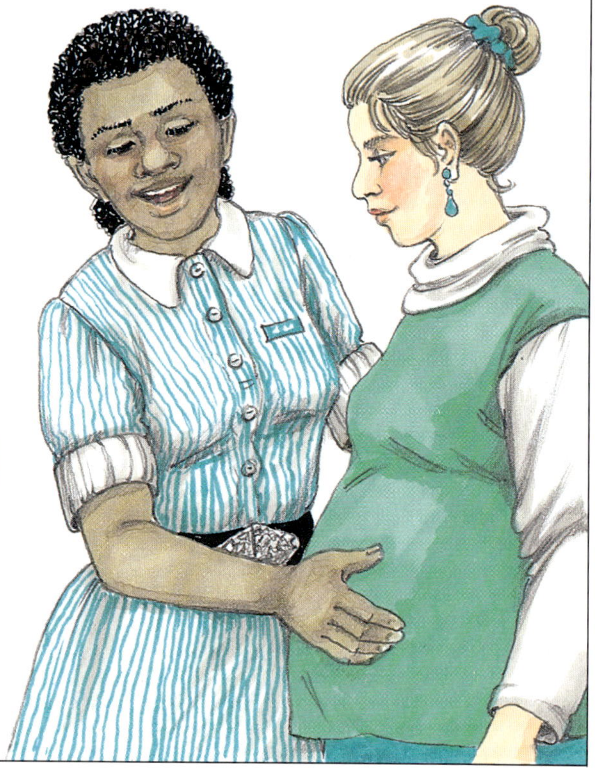

Twice a week there is a clinic for babies. The health visitor weighs the babies to make sure they are growing properly and discusses any problems with the parents.

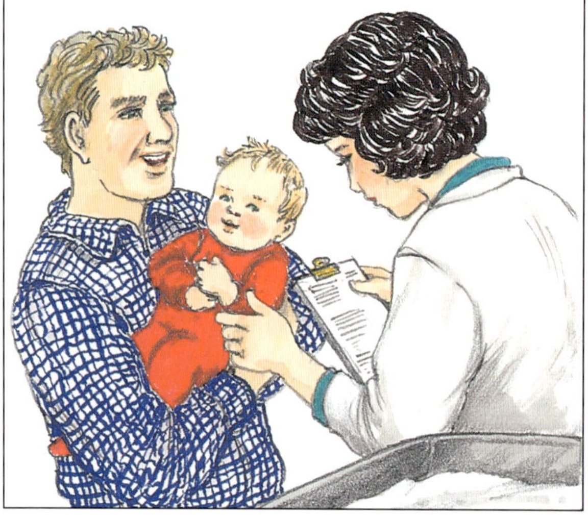

When morning surgery is over, the doctor sets off on her rounds. She visits people who cannot come to the surgery. Some are too ill or too old, others have illnesses such as chicken pox and mumps which spread to other people very easily.

There might be an emergency while the doctor is on her rounds. The doctor has a phone in her car so she can be reached at all times.

In the afternoon, the doctor goes back to the surgery. Once again, there are a lot of patients for her to see.

The doctors take it in turns to be 'on call' at home when the surgery is closed. The doctor on call carries a bleeper if she has to go out. If the bleeper sounds, the doctor has to phone a special number to find out where she is needed. She may be called out at any time.

More about: infectious illness pp24, 30 X-ray pp17, 33, 44-45

Going to hospital

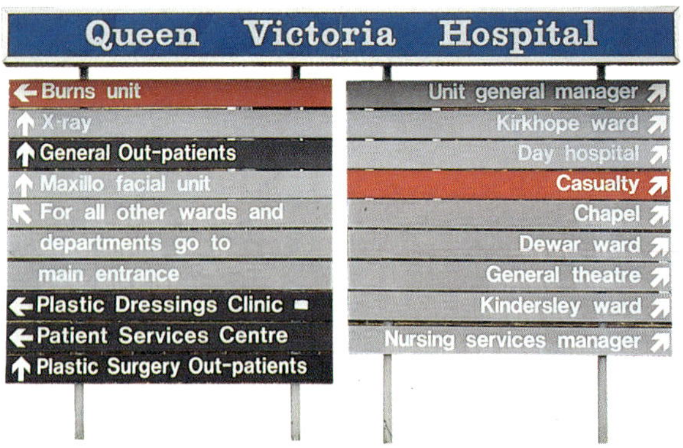

Large hospitals have several different departments, often in different buildings. Many hospital patients have to stay there for a few days or even weeks. They may need an operation. They may have to be kept under observation so that the doctors can find out what is wrong with them.

Out-patients

Some patients visit the hospital only for an X-ray. Others need treatment such as having a broken bone set. These people visit the hospital as **out-patients**. Some cases are dealt with by the hospital's accident and emergency unit (casualty). People can also visit specialists as out-patients.

Visiting casualty

The casualty department has a large waiting area. Several receptionists work in an office behind a counter. Patients usually go to casualty for something their own doctor cannot treat at the surgery, such as a broken bone.

1

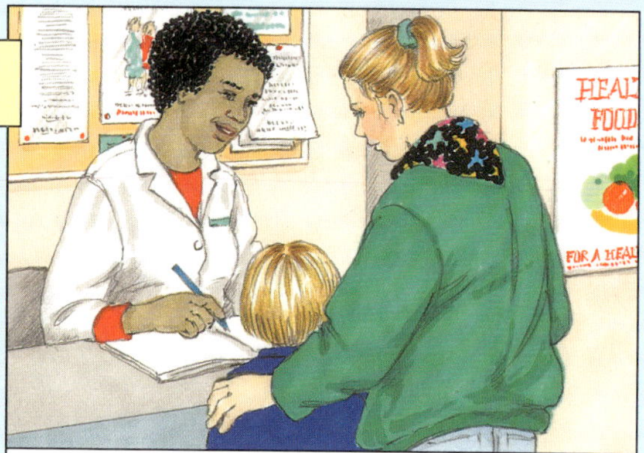

Patients go to see a receptionist as soon as they arrive. She asks them what is wrong and makes some notes for the doctor. Then she sends them to sit in the waiting area.

Hospitals also have to deal with sudden emergencies such as injuries caused by road accidents. These patients are rushed to casualty, usually by ambulance.

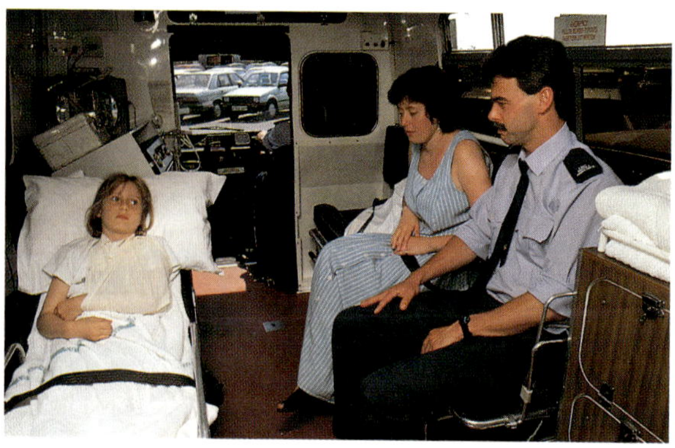

2

The casualty department is usually very busy. People with serious injuries have to be treated urgently, but there may be a long wait for other patients.

3

There are several small rooms where doctors see patients. A nurse talks to a patient first to find out what is wrong, who their own doctor is and other information which the hospital needs.

4

A doctor examines the patient and decides what treatment to give. An X-ray may be needed. The doctor studies the X-ray pictures and discusses treatment with the patient.

5

Sometimes a patient has to be admitted into the hospital. This may be because the doctor wants to check that there are no delayed reactions to an injury.

More about: broken bones pp16, 19 operation pp17, 48-49 X-ray pp17, 33

Seeing a specialist

A hospital has several different units which specialise in different types of treatment.

A woman who is having a baby goes to the **maternity** unit.

The **geriatric** unit cares for old people.

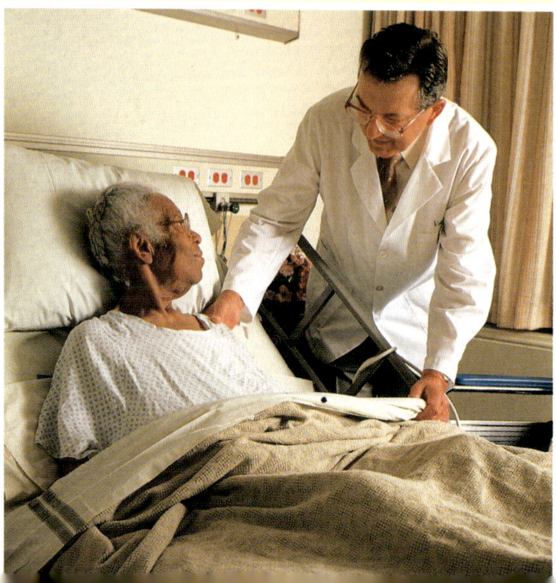

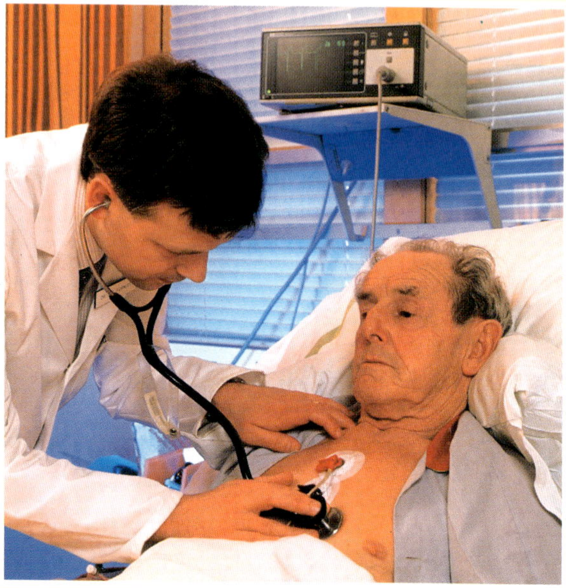

Someone with heart problems goes to the **cardiology** unit.

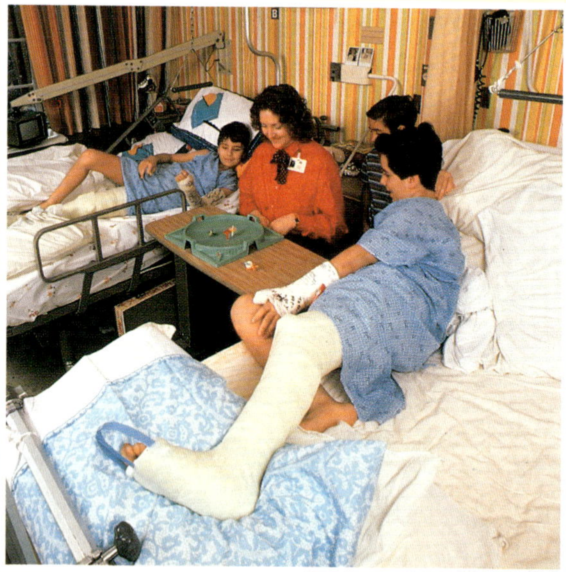

The **paediatric** unit specialises in children's illnesses.

A child who keeps getting tonsillitis would be sent to the ENT (Ear, Nose and Throat) unit.

Consultants

Each unit has a specialist doctor in charge. These specialists are called **consultants**. Unless patients have been rushed into hospital for some reason, they usually see a consultant as an out-patient. If they have to be admitted into hospital, the consultant sees them in the wards and decides on the treatment they should have. Each unit also has junior doctors who see to the day-to-day treatment of patients.

Patients are sent to see a specialist by their GP. The specialist examines the patient in the same way as the GP does. He can get in touch with the patient's GP to give his opinion and recommend treatment. If necessary, he can have the patient admitted to the hospital.

How many different units does your local hospital have? What do they do?

Physiotherapy

The physiotherapy unit is a specialist department where disorders or injuries are treated by **physical** methods. These include **massage**, heat treatment, and exercise.

If treatment is painful, physiotherapy is sometimes carried out in a swimming pool. The patient's body floats in the water which takes some of the load off the limbs. It is easier to exercise in water because the limbs are supported by the water.

Arthritis is a painful condition in which the joints swell up and become stiff. Physiotherapy can help relieve the pain and stiffness.

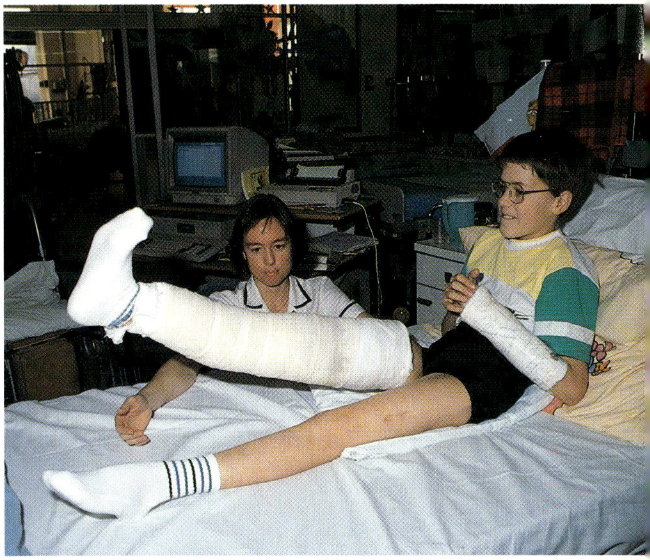

*Patients are sometimes sent for physiotherapy after a **fracture**. The physiotherapist gives them exercises to strengthen muscles.*

Heat treatment helps strained muscles and also relieves joint and muscle pain. Massage is mainly used to ease pains in the muscles.

More about: heart disease pp52-53 water exercise pp17

The surgeon

Sometimes a patient needs an operation to remove a diseased part of the body or replace or repair a damaged part. An operation, or surgery, is performed by a specially trained doctor called a surgeon.

The surgeon works with a team of people which includes an anaesthetist, specially trained nurses and some technicians to operate equipment.

Surgery ranges from minor operations such as removing a wart to major operations such as heart transplants. Many surgeons specialise in a particular area of the body such as the heart, the brain, the eyes, or the bones. Other surgeons, known as general surgeons, carry out a variety of operations such as removing an appendix or tonsils.

Having an operation

While the patient is in the **ward**, she is dressed in a long hospital gown. She is then given an injection to make her feel relaxed and drowsy. This is called a 'pre-med', which is short for premedication.

1

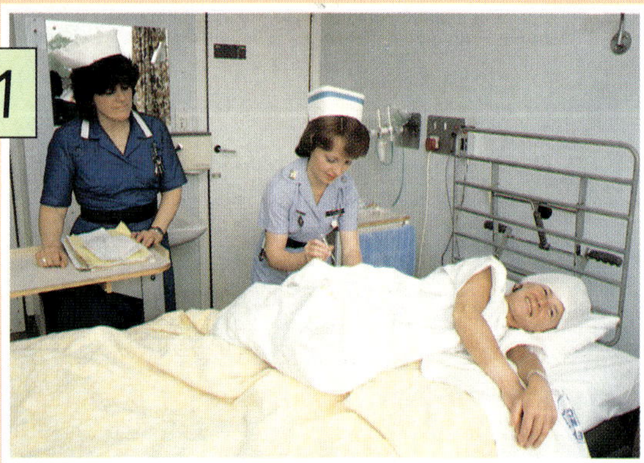

For some minor operations, the patient has a local anaesthetic. She is awake during the operation, but the part being operated on is numbed.

2

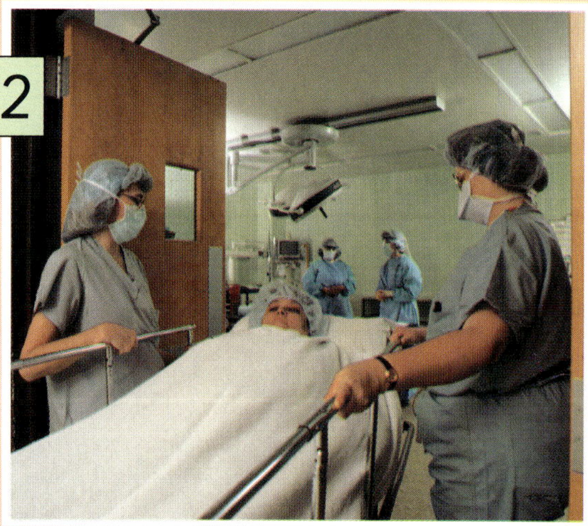

Before the operation, the patient is given an anaesthetic to stop her feeling any pain. The anaesthetic is usually given by injection. With a general anaesthetic, the patient is put into a deep sleep. She must not eat or drink for several hours before the operation because she might be sick. The patient is then wheeled into the operating theatre.

3

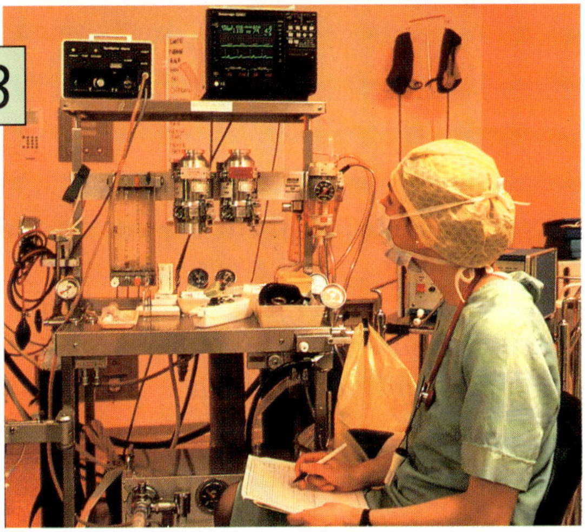

During the operation, the anaesthetist checks that the patient remains unconscious and that there are no problems.

It is important that no micro-organisms can get into the operating theatre to infect the patient. Everyone in the team wears a gown, cap, gloves, rubber boots and mask. Everything must be **sterilised** before it is used.

4

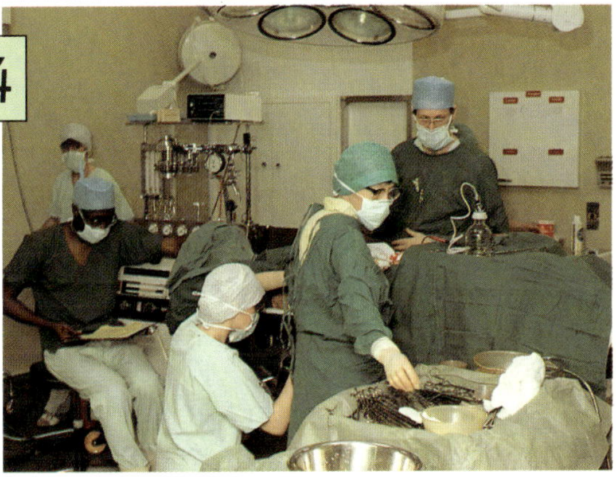

The surgeon uses a scalpel for cutting, and forceps which are like tweezers. A nurse hands the surgeon each instrument as he asks for it.

5

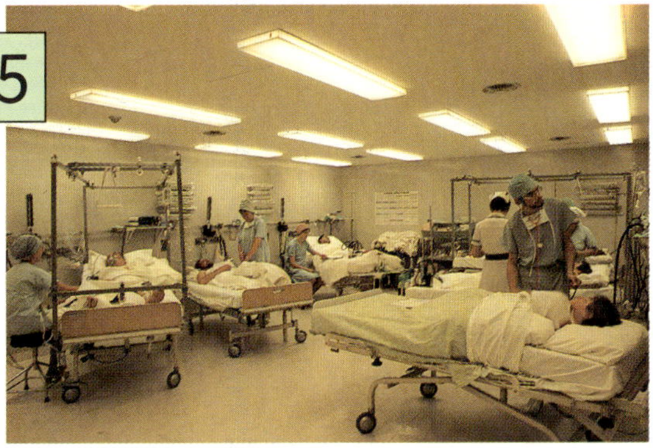

When the operation is over, the anaesthetist gives the patient another drug to make her wake up. She is wheeled into the recovery room where she wakes up after a few minutes. Then she is taken back to the ward.

The patient may feel a bit sick after the anaesthetic. She will also feel sore. Nurses on the ward give her pain-killing drugs. Lying in bed makes the muscles stiff, so the patient should get up and move around as soon as possible.

Did you know...?

About 150 years ago, operations were carried out without any anaesthetic in unhygienic conditions. Many patients died. The first operation under a general anaesthetic was performed in Massachusetts, USA, in 1846. Patients breathed in a gas called ether, which put them to sleep.

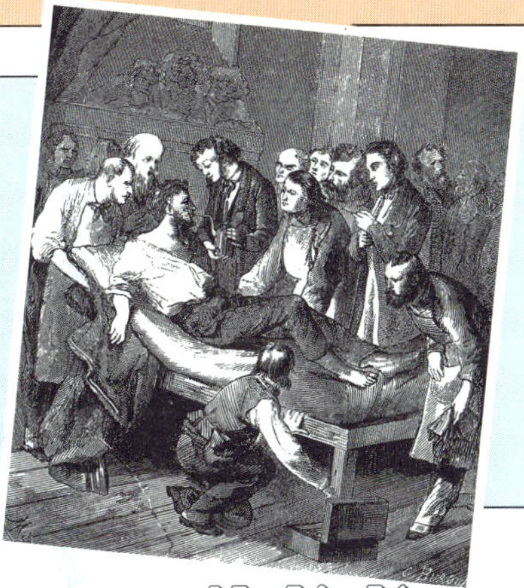

More about: micro-organisms pp4, 10, 25, 35 surgery pp15, 54, 56

Major surgery

Major operations involve very skilled work and can take several hours to perform.

What can go wrong with your body?

EYES
Eye surgery is very delicate. Glaucoma is an illness where **fluid** presses on the eye and damages the nerves. If it is not treated, the sufferer will gradually go blind. Surgery is sometimes needed to drain fluid from the eye.

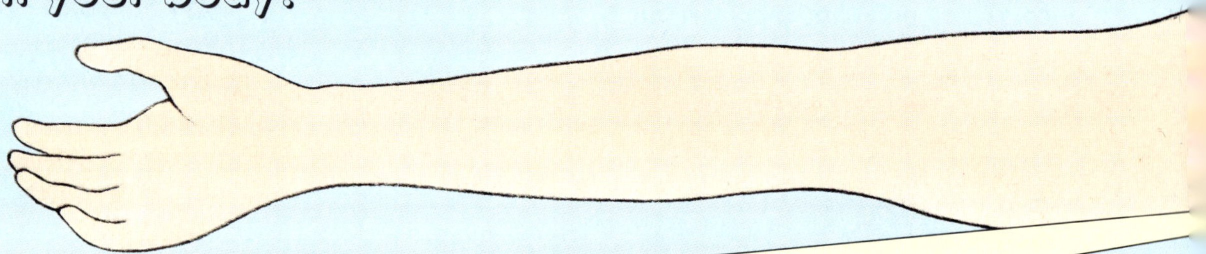

LUNGS
These are the main organs of the breathing system. They can become infected, but most illnesses can be cured with antibiotics. The most serious illness is lung cancer, which is often caused by smoking cigarettes. If the cancer is found early enough, the diseased part of the lung can be removed by surgery.

HEART
This pumps blood round your body. A diseased heart can be replaced in a heart transplant. Other heart operations include open heart surgery. In this the heart is opened and repaired. A heart bypass treats blocked arteries. Faulty valves leading to the heart can be replaced by surgery.

KIDNEYS
These help to clean your blood by removing waste products. Some people are born with kidney defects. Kidney failure can be caused by shock after an accident, or by disease. Sometimes stones, or hard lumps, form in the kidneys. An operation may be needed to remove a large stone.

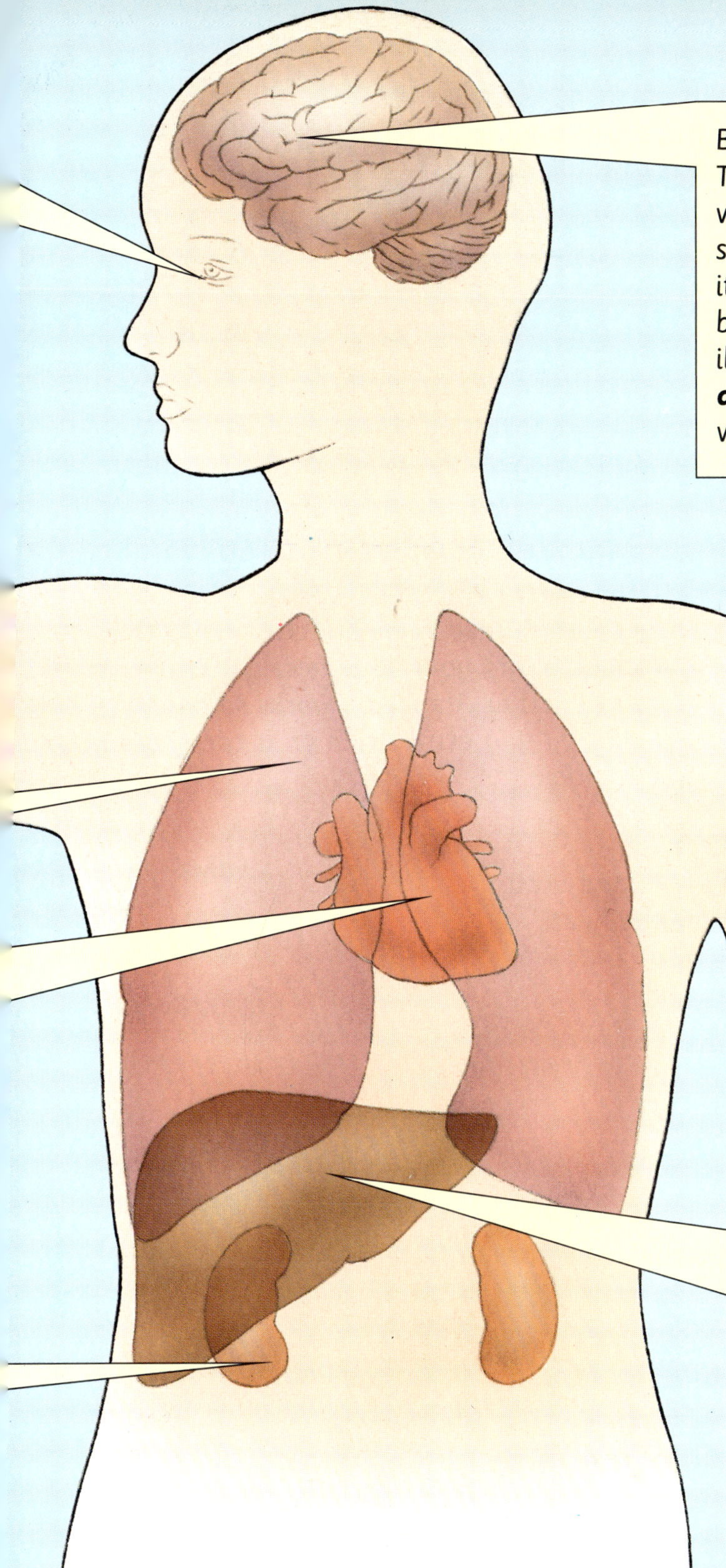

BRAIN
This sends and receives messages which control everything you do. It is surrounded by the skull which protects it, but makes operating difficult. The brain can become infected, causing illnesses such as meningitis or an **abscess**. A brain tumour is a growth which has to be removed by surgery.

LIVER
This releases **nutrients** from food into the bloodstream and clears the blood of harmful substances. Liver problems include tumours, infections such as hepatitis, and diseases caused by drinking too much alcohol. People are sometimes born with liver defects.

More about: heart transplant pp56 lung cancer pp39

What causes heart conditions?

Heart disorders are the most common cause of death in Europe and America. Heart diseases can be genetic. People whose families have a history of heart disorders are more likely to suffer from a heart disorder themselves.

. Some babies are born with heart defects, but these are not usually genetic. They are caused by the baby developing wrongly in the mother's womb. Slight defects may disappear as the baby gets older. Others can be corrected by surgery.

How the heart works

The heart never stops working. It beats about 70 times a minute and pumps the blood round your body nearly 3000 times a day. The heart works so hard that putting extra strain on it can cause it to fail.

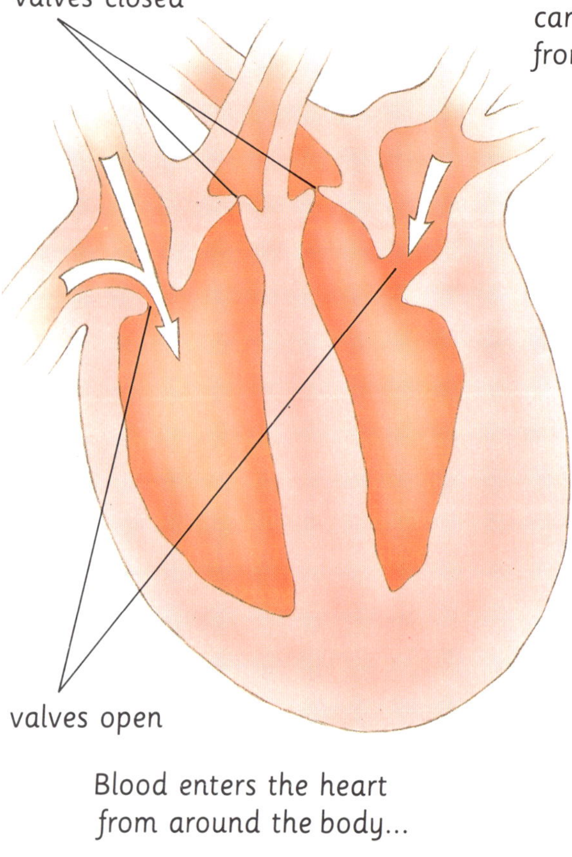

Blood enters the heart from around the body...

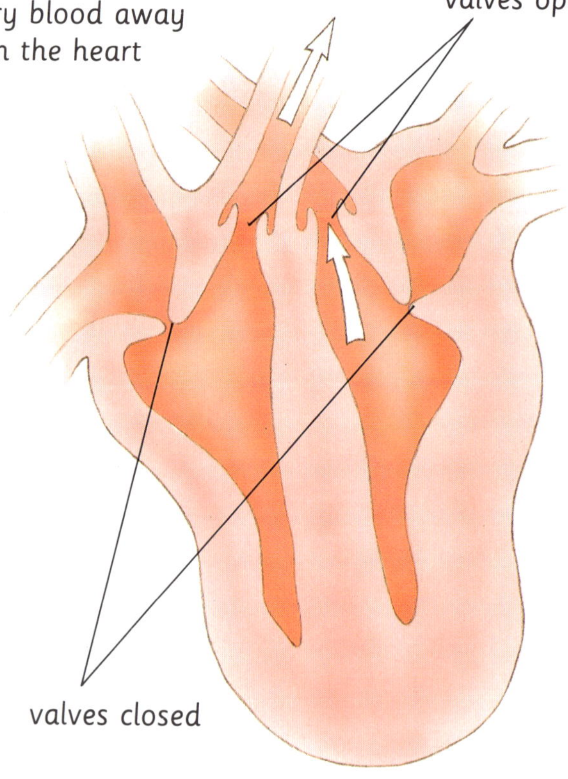

...and is pumped out again.

Too many fatty foods are bad for you because fat clogs the arteries. The channel becomes narrower and the heart has to work very hard to pump the blood through.

High blood pressure

People who are overweight are putting a strain on the heart. They often suffer from high blood pressure. If the arteries are narrowed by fat, the heart has to pump the blood with greater force. High blood pressure can also be caused by smoking, stress, drinking too much alcohol and not taking enough exercise.

Lifestyle

Many heart disorders are caused by a person's lifestyle. Modern life is very stressful.

They worry about paying their bills or keeping their jobs.

Many people work in noisy offices and factories.

People forget how to relax.

They eat hurried meals...

Perhaps they drive there through heavy traffic...

... and find it difficult to 'switch off' and go to sleep at night.

... or travel on crowded trains.

Stress makes the heart beat faster, putting it under constant strain.

More about: alcohol pp25, 39 exercise pp17, 54-55 smoking pp39, 50, 55

After an operation

Somebody who has just had a serious operation such as heart surgery has to be very careful. As well as recovering from the operation itself, the patient has to make sure that he or she does not go back to any habits that may have caused the illness in the first place.

A good diet

Heart patients usually have to keep to a good diet. This way they keep their weight down and avoid eating too much fat.

A heart patient is encouraged to take some exercise to strengthen the heart. This should not be too strenuous or it could strain the heart again.

High fibre foods such as wholewheat bread, brown rice, cereals, fruit and vegetables help to keep weight down. They help to push waste materials through the body. They also prevent too much fat and sugar from getting into the bloodstream too quickly. Fibre foods are 'filling' so you feel satisfied after the meal.

Did you know...?

Heavy smokers are four times more likely to suffer from heart disease than non-smokers.

As well as fatty foods, too many sugary foods such as cakes and biscuits make people put on weight.

It is dangerous for anyone with a heart condition to smoke cigarettes. The nicotine in cigarettes increases blood pressure and also makes the heart beat faster. This puts a double strain on the heart. Cigarette smoking can double the risk of dying from a heart attack.

Learning to relax

People should try to avoid stress and worry. People may be able to lessen the stresses of everyday life by making sure that there is time for rest and relaxation. Exercise, fresh air and sleep help people to relax and cope with stress.

More about: diet pp4, 29 exercise pp11, 17, 53 relaxation pp25

Transplant surgery

Until the mid-1960s, patients who had badly diseased organs usually died. Then it was discovered that a diseased organ could be removed and replaced with a healthy one.

Today, hearts, livers, lungs, kidneys, **bone marrow** and the **cornea** of the eye can all be transplanted. However, transplant operations are still a fairly new idea and they do not always succeed.

Finding a donor

Before a transplant can be carried out, a replacement organ has to be found. These organs usually come from young, healthy people who have died from other causes, such as a road accident. The organ must be transplanted quickly or it will not start working again. Patients sometimes die because a **donor** cannot be found in time.

Hospitals keep all the details of patients waiting for transplants on a computer. When a donor organ becomes available, doctors can quickly check who it would be most suitable for.

The organs of the donor and the patient must match very closely. Otherwise, the patient's body will reject the new organ. It treats the organ as an 'invader' and destroys it in the same way that it destroys micro-organisms.

Even if the organ is a good match, the body may try to reject it. Doctors can now give patients drugs which prevent this happening.

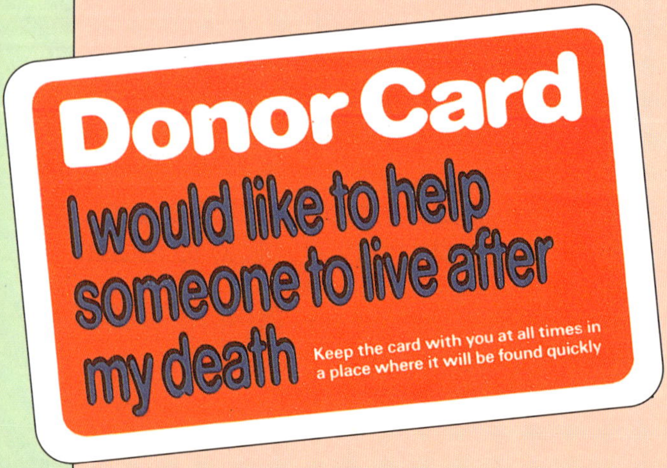

People who want to help others live, after they die, carry donor cards. These cards let doctors know that their organs can be used in transplant operations.

Artificial parts

Some parts of the body can be replaced with artificial 'spares'.

Artificial limbs have joints and can bend like real limbs.

Joints such as the hip and knee become worn with age. They may need to be replaced with artificial joints. They are usually made of plastic. People who have to have an arm or a leg **amputated** can be fitted with an artificial limb.

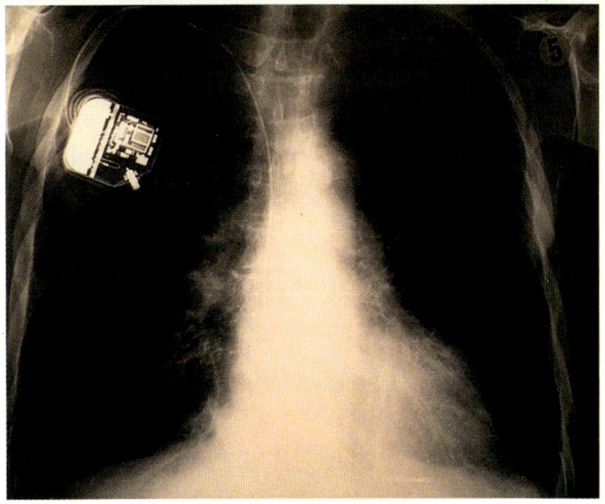

This X-ray shows a 'pacemaker' in position in the body. Pacemakers are fitted in people with some heart conditions. In a healthy heart, the heartbeat is kept up by **impulses** to the heart muscle. A pacemaker supplies the heart with electrical impulses if the heart is not providing its own properly.

A gift of life

Sometimes organs can be taken from a living person. For example, you have two kidneys but you can live a normal life with only one. Sometimes a person gives a kidney to save the life of someone with kidney disease. Bone marrow can also be taken from a living person, often a close relative of the patient.

Did you know...?

- *The first heart transplant was carried out in South Africa in 1967 by a medical team headed by Dr Christian Barnard.*
- *The first heart-lung-liver transplant took place in 1986 at Papworth Hospital in England.*

More about: heart pp50, 52-53 kidneys pp7, 50 micro-organisms pp10, 25

Blood groups

Sometimes people lose blood in accidents or during an operation. They can be given a blood transfusion to replace this blood.

If you cut yourself, you bleed. Your blood looks the same as anyone else's, but there are many different blood types. Blood types have to be matched in blood transfusions. The first blood transfusions were carried out, in the 19th century. Some were successful, but others led to serious illness and sometimes death. This made doctors realise that blood types did not always mix.

Hospitals may need blood at any time. They store supplies of all the different blood groups in blood banks. The blood is stored at 1–6 °C in refrigerators. The blood comes from healthy adults who have ***volunteered*** *to give it.*

Blood is made up of red cells, which carry ***oxygen*** *around the body, and white cells which fight off micro-organisms. Blood groups are identified by the type of red cells. The main groups are called A, B, AB and O. The chart shows which blood types can or cannot be mixed. (The donor is the person* giving *blood and the recipient is the person* receiving *blood).*

From this chart, you can see that a person with group O blood has to be given group O blood in a transfusion. But they can give blood to any of the other groups. A person with AB blood can receive any type, but can only give blood to another AB person. What blood group are you? If you have B blood, who can you give blood to? Who can you receive blood from?

		Donor blood group			
		A	**B**	**AB**	**O**
Recipient blood group	**A**	✔	✘	✘	✔
	B	✘	✔	✘	✔
	AB	✔	✔	✔	✔
	O	✘	✘	✘	✔

Giving blood

The human body contains about 5 litres of blood. If you lose a fairly small amount of this, your body can make it up again quite quickly. You may not feel any effects at all, though some people feel a little sick and faint for a few minutes after giving blood.

Did you know...?

- The most common blood group in the world is O. In the UK, A is the most common group, followed by O, then B and lastly AB.
- The rarest blood is in a group called Bombay blood. So far this has been found in only three people in the world.

1 Blood donors give blood regularly, usually twice a year, at a hospital or a blood donor centre.

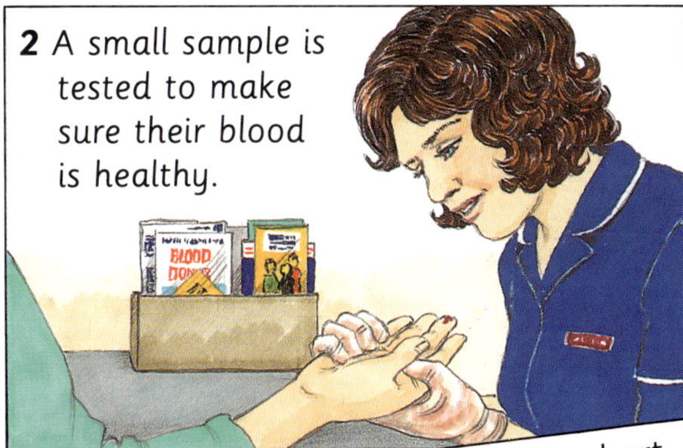

2 A small sample is tested to make sure their blood is healthy.

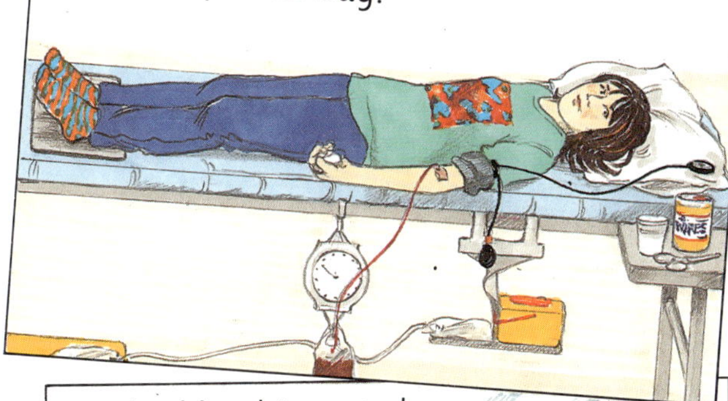

3 A needle is put into their arm and about 500 ml of blood is drawn out into a plastic bag.

4 Donors rest for a short while before going home. They are told not to do anything too strenuous for a few hours. This gives their bodies time to build up supplies of blood.

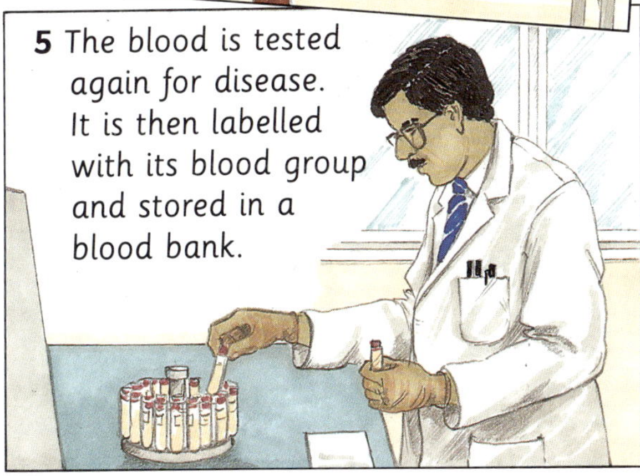

5 The blood is tested again for disease. It is then labelled with its blood group and stored in a blood bank.

6 You may think that blood banks build up huge supplies in this way, but blood keeps for only three or four weeks. Then it has to be thrown away if it has not been used.

More about: blood test pp27 micro-organisms pp4, 10, 25

Getting better

Patients recovering from an operation or illness stay in the wards until they are well enough to go home. Several nurses work on each ward with a senior nurse in charge. They work in 'shifts', some in the daytime, others at night.

A hospital day

1 The patients are woken up early in the morning. The nurses start their rounds, taking temperatures and pulses. They also give medicines prescribed by doctors.

2 Then breakfast arrives. Meals come round on trolleys. The patients can usually order what they want from two or three choices. Some patients have to stay on a strict diet so the doctor decides what they can eat.

3 Nurses bring bedpans to patients who cannot get up to go to the toilet.

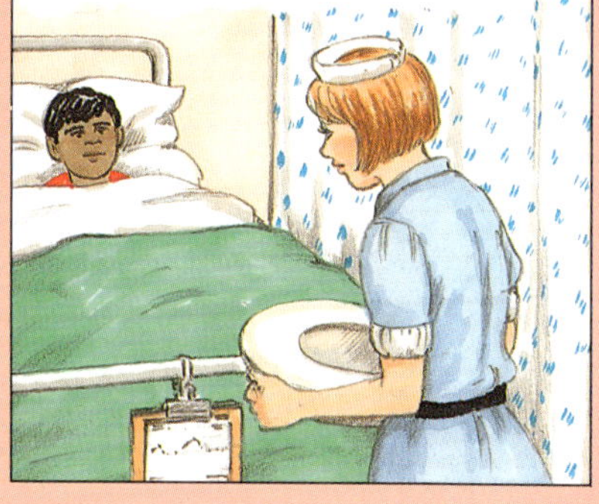

4 They also wash the patients who are too ill to get out of bed. Patients who are well enough can go to a bathroom to wash or have a bath.

5 The nurses then remake all the beds in the ward.

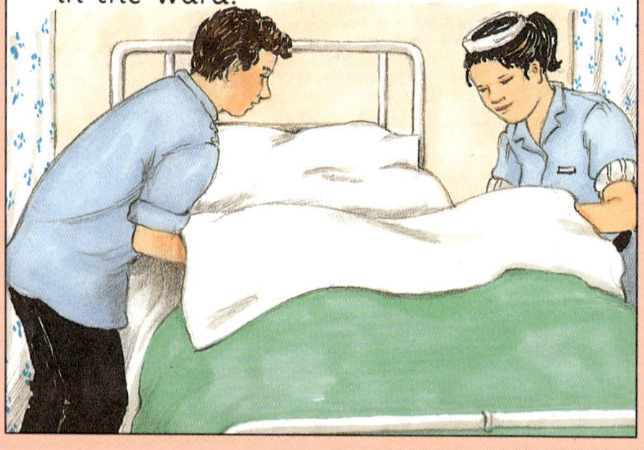

6 The consultant and junior doctors come round in the morning. In a teaching hospital, medical students often come round with the consultant.

7 Each patient has a chart where the doctors and nurses make notes. If there is an emergency, anyone can see quickly how the patient is being treated.

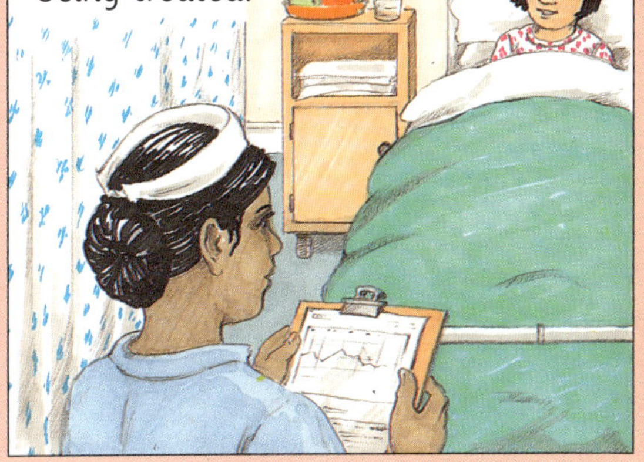

8 Some patients have to stay in bed. Others are well enough to get up and walk around. There is a room where they can sit and watch television or chat. Children's wards have rooms with toys for the children to play with.

9 Some hospitals have special visiting times when friends and relatives can visit patients. This is often in the afternoon or evening, when the routine work of the wards has been completed. Other hospitals allow visitors at any time. Sometimes the visitors bring presents for the patient.

More about: doctors pp5, 24-25, 40-43 nurses pp42, 48 pulse pp32

Key words

The meanings of words can depend on how and when they are used. You may find that as you learn more about science the meanings change slightly.

abscess a collection of pus formed as a result of infection by micro-organisms

allergy a condition caused by the body's reaction to a certain substance

amplifies makes larger or greater

amputated removed

anaesthetic a drug which puts a patient to sleep or numbs a part of the body so that no pain is felt

anaesthetist a person who is qualified to give anaesthetics

antibiotic a drug that kills bacteria, but does not harm body cells

antitoxin a substance which acts against a poison and makes it harmless

arteries tubes in the body which carry blood away from the heart

arthritis inflammation of a joint which causes pain, swelling and stiffness

bacteria a group of micro-organisms, some of which cause disease

blood pressure the force with which the heart pumps blood round the body

blood transfusion giving a person a large amount of new blood

bone marrow soft substance at the centre of a bone where blood cells are made

bronchii small air passages which connect the windpipe to the lungs

cardiology the study of the way in which the heart works, diagnosis and treatment of heart conditions

cell one of the tiny 'building blocks' that make up our bodies

clots joins together and stops flowing

consultant a doctor who specialises in a particular branch of medicine

contagious passed on by personal contact

contaminated polluted or infected

cornea transparent covering of the eyeball

counselling advice and support given by a professional person to help someone cope with a problem

dependent unable to do without

diagnose to find out what is wrong with someone

diet the different foods we eat

digestive system the parts of the body which break down food

donor a person who gives, or donates, something

drugs substances which change the way one or more body organs work, or change the course of an illness. Drugs include medicines and non-medical substances such as tobacco and alcohol

endoscope an instrument for looking inside the body

energy the ability to do a job

environment surroundings

epidemic a sudden and rapid spread of a disease, affecting large numbers of people

extinct an animal or plant that has died out

fatal leading to death

fertilise to join a sperm from a male with an egg from a female so that a baby grows

fibre optic transmitting images through bundles of thin flexible glass or plastic threads

fluid a substance which moves freely such as a liquid

fracture a break in a bone

fungi micro-organisms such as mushrooms, toadstools or mould

general practitioner a doctor who provides general medical care outside a hospital

genes tiny parts of each cell which affect what a living thing looks like and the way in which it develops

genetic caused by genes

geriatric elderly

hepatitis inflammation of the liver

immune resistant to a disease because the body can fight off invading micro-organisms

impulses short, regular bursts of energy

infectious able to be passed from one person to another

infested to be overrun by troublesome things such as insects or rats

inherit to receive qualities or characteristics from parents

jaundice a disorder of the liver which causes the skin and whites of the eyes to turn yellow

mammals warm-blooded animals covered with hair and which have a backbone; most give birth to live young and produce milk to feed them

massage rubbing and kneading areas of the body, usually with the hands

maternity having a baby; the branch of medicine concerned with childbirth

micro-organism a very tiny living thing which can only be seen with a microscope; some micro-organisms cause disease

nutrients substances which provide food for a living thing

orthopaedic the branch of medicine concerned with disorders of bones and joints

out-patients patients who visit a hospital for treatment but do not stay there

overdose more than the recommended dose

oxygen one of the gases in the air

paediatrics the branch of medicine concerned with the growth and development of children

parasite a plant or animal which lives on another

pedigree bred from a known line of animals of the same species

penicillin antibiotic discovered by Alexander Fleming in 1928

pharmacist person who prepares medicines

physical of, or concerned with, the body

plankton tiny plants or animals that float in seas, lakes and rivers

pollution spoiling of the environment by people

prescription a written instruction from a doctor telling a chemist to give a patient a particular drug

preserved prevented from going bad by special preparation such as pickling

primates the highest group of mammals, which includes people, apes and monkeys

pulse the heartbeat felt as blood throbbing through an artery

quarantine a period of time when a person or animal is kept away from others to avoid spreading disease

radiographer a person who is qualified to take X-rays

sterilised free from micro-organisms

stethoscope an instrument for listening to sounds inside the body, particularly those in the heart and lungs

stress a feeling of strain and worry

symptoms signs or indications of an illness

tranquillisers drugs for relieving stress

vaccinate inject with a vaccine that makes the body resistant to a disease

valves structures that allow blood to flow in one direction through a tube or passageway, but close to prevent it from flowing in the other direction

virus the smallest known type of living thing which causes disease

volunteered offered to do something

ward a hospital room containing two or more beds, where patients recover from operations or illness

withdrawal symptoms the body's reaction when a drug that it is dependent on is taken away

X-rays rays which can penetrate the body but are absorbed by the bones; a photograph of the inside of part of the body

Index

alcohol 25, 39, 53
allergies 26
anaemia 29
anaesthetic 17, 48–9
analgesics 36
animal sanctuaries 18–19
antibiotics 10, 21, 36
antitoxin 35
arthritis 47
artificial parts 57
asthma 26
athlete's foot 25

bacteria 4, 10, 34–5
Barnard, Dr Christian 57
birds 6
blood 7, 29, 58–9
blood donors 59
blood groups 58–9
blood pressure 32–3, 53
botulism 35
brain 7, 51
breeding 12–13
broken bones 5, 11, 17

casualty 44–5
childhood illnesses 30
cigarettes 25, 39, 53
colds 25, 30
colic 15, 17
colour blindness 27
consultants 47, 61
contagious illnesses 25, 30
Cook, Captain 29

diagnosis 5, 32–3
diet 4, 22, 25, 29, 53, 54–5, 60
distemper 8
doctors 5, 24–5, 40–3, 61
drug abuse 38–9
drugs 36–9

eczema 26
Elizabethan collar 14
endoscope 33
exercise 11, 17, 25, 53, 54
extinct animals 23
eye surgery 50

Falabella horse 13
feline infectious enteritis 8
Fleming, Alexander 36
flu 25, 30
fly strike 11
food poisoning 34–5
fungi 4, 10, 25

general practitioner 24, 40–3
genes 25, 26
genetic disorders 25, 26–7

haemoglobin 29
haemophilia 27
hay fever 26
health visitor 42
heart 7, 50, 52
heart disease 39, 52–3
heart transplant 50, 56, 57
hepatitis 11
Hippocrates 5
hospital 44–9, 56–61
hospital units 46–7
hospital ward 60–1
hygiene 34

infectious illnesses 25, 30, 31
inspection of new pet 6–7

jaundice 11
Jenner. Edward 31

kidneys 7, 50

liver 7, 11, 51
lung cancer 39, 51
lungs 7, 50

malaria 28
mammals 6–7
micro-organisms 4, 11, 49
midwife 42
mongrels 12
muscles 7

neutering 13
nurses 16, 42, 49, 60
nutrients 7, 29

oiled birds 19
operations 15, 17, 48–51
organs 6–7, 50–1
out-patients 44

parasites 9, 28
pedigree animals 12
penicillin 36
pharmacists 36
physiotherapy 47
polio 30–1
prescriptions 36, 38
pulse 32, 60

quarantine 20

relaxation 55
reproduction 13, 26
reptile hospitals 17
rickets 29

Salmonella 35
scurvy 29
seals 19, 22
skeleton 7
sleeping sickness 28
smallpox 31
specialists 46–7
stress 21, 53
surgeons 48–9

temperature 32, 60
tonsillitis 41
tranquillisers 38
transplants 50, 56–7

vaccination 8, 14, 30–1
veterinary hospitals 16, 17
vets 5, 6–17, 18, 23
viruses 4, 10, 25, 30–1

wildlife sanctuaries 19
worming 9, 21
wounds 5, 11, 14

X-rays 16, 41, 45

zoos 20–3